INSPIRE / PLAN / DISCOVER / EXPERIENCE

UMBRIA

UMBRIA

CONTENTS

DISCOVER 6

EXPERIENCE 58

NEED TO KNOW 172

Left: Staircase in Deruta decorated with ceramics
Previous page: Autumnal vineyards near Montefalco
Front cover: Looking down at Spello's Porta Venere

DISCOVER

Looking out over the city of Spoleto

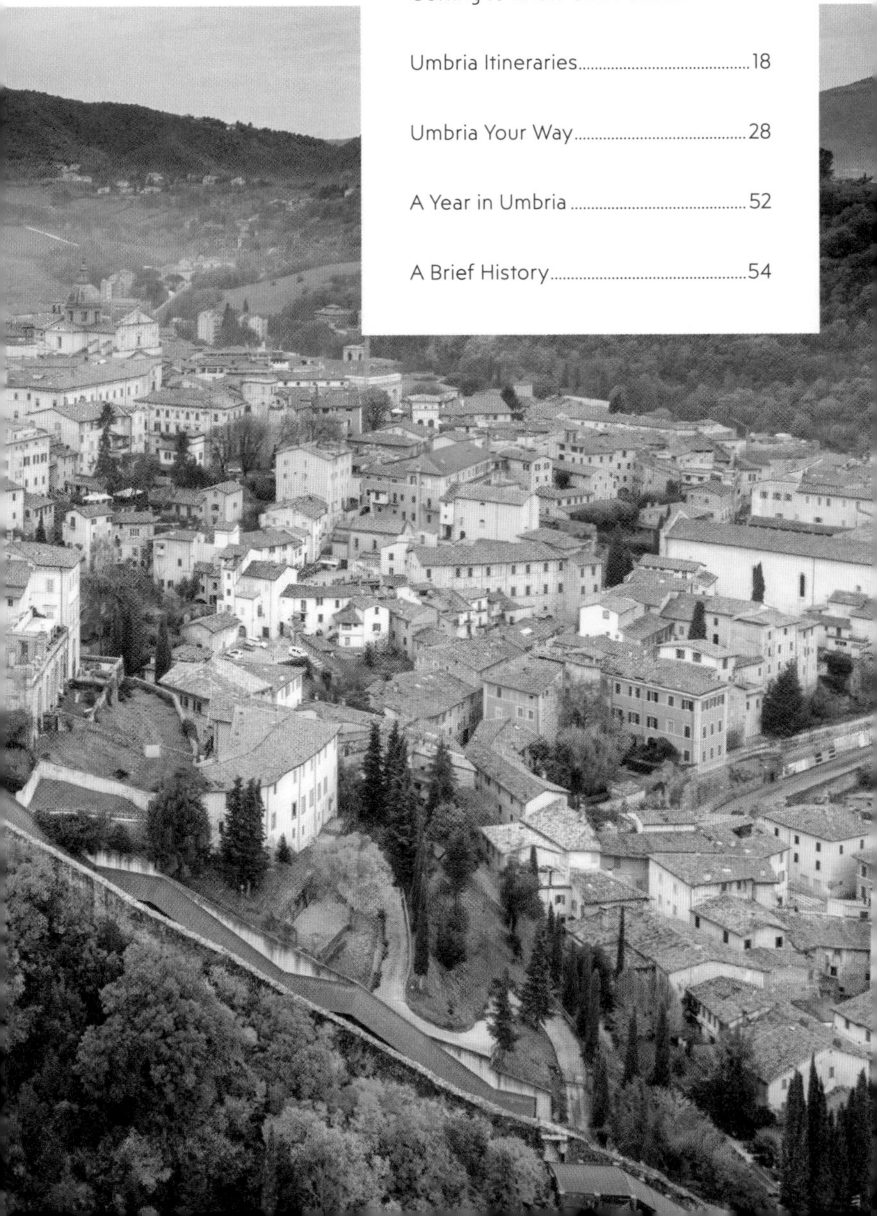

WELCOME TO
UMBRIA

Undulating hills sprinkled with leafy vineyards. Enchanting hilltop towns home to stunning, fresco-filled churches and medieval fortresses. Freshly foraged, seasonal food and locally made wine. Umbria has it all. Whatever your dream trip to this Italian region includes, this DK Eyewitness travel guide is the perfect companion.

1 Wildflowers next to Castelluccio di Norcia.

2 Gubbio's Festa dei Ceri.

3 Passignano sul Trasimeno, a pretty village on Lago Trasimeno.

4 The bustling Piazza IV Novembre in Perugia.

Tucked away in the middle of Italy, landlocked Umbria is a bucolic region known for its rolling hills and gently sloping valleys, dotted with a patchwork of lush fields, ancient olive groves and verdant vineyards. Beyond this picture of pastoral perfection lie rushing rivers, twinkling lakes and mountainous peaks, some of which sit within protected parks. Elsewhere, fertile plains bloom with colourful wildflowers, while pockets of woodland are the realm of mushrooms and truffles – prizes for local foragers.

Strewn across this varied landscape are charming hilltop towns and cities, which burst with art and culture. Chief among them is the region's capital, Perugia, famed for its world-class art gallery, and rose-coloured Assisi, home to a majestic, fresco-filled basilica and imposing fortress. These towns and cities are the perfect place to feast, whether you're devouring plates of truffle-topped pasta or sipping on a glass of the region's world-class wine. History also has a strong pull, with everything from Roman-era towns to underground Etruscan labyrinths found here. The region loves festivals, too, with medieval re-enactments, chocolate-tasting events, cool jazz performances and more taking place throughout the year.

Umbria is filled with such a variety of sights that it can be hard to know where to start. We've broken the region down into easily navigable chapters, with detailed itineraries, expert local knowledge and colourful, comprehensive maps to help you plan the perfect trip. However long you plan to stay, this DK Eyewitness travel guide will ensure that you see the best of this spectacular region. Enjoy the book, and enjoy Umbria.

REASONS TO LOVE
UMBRIA

Undulating emerald-gold hills and sapphire-blue lakes. Feudal castles and fortified hilltowns. Religious masterpieces and ancient ruins. There are so many reasons to love Umbria; here are a few of our favourites.

1 ITALY'S GREEN HEART
The region is famed for its lush greenery, from rolling hills dotted with vineyards, to the forested valleys and emerald peaks of regional parks like the Parco Regionale del Monte Cucco (p68).

VINEYARDS GALORE 2
Umbria's rich soil and sunny Mediterranean climate produce some of the world's best wines. Drop by a local vineyard, such as Tenuta Bellafonte (p133), for tours and tastings.

3 FESTIVALS
Religious parades, foodie feasts and performing arts events: Umbria is awash with incredible festivals. Don't miss one of the region's medieval re-enactments, such as Assisi's Calendimaggio (p52).

WONDERFUL WALKS *4*

Whether you're into gentle ambles or epic hikes, Umbria offers countless opportunities to explore on foot. Follow in St Francis' footsteps *(p94)*, stroll beside the River Tiber *(p90)* or summit Monte Subasio *(p112)*.

BEAUTIFUL BLOOMS *5*

Umbria has plenty of petal power. Wander Assisi's pretty geranium-lined streets *(p102)* or spy the annual display of multicoloured wildflowers at Castelluccio di Norcia *(p148)*.

SLOW-FOOD SCENE *6*

For Umbrians, eating locally and seasonally has been a way of life for centuries. Go foraging for your own ingredients *(p51)* or let a local chef rustle up a farm-fresh dish.

LAGO TRASIMENO 7

This beautiful lake *(p76)* is the largest in Umbria. Its teal waters are dotted with forested islands, while its shores are home to a number of picturesque villages.

MEDIEVAL HILLTOWNS 8

The likes of Orvieto *(p124)* and Todi *(p120)* take you on a journey back in time. Amble along cobbled streets, peer over rampart-capped walls and explore historic palaces.

9 AGRITURISMOS

For an unhurried taste of the rural good life, spend some time at a farmstay. Some offer courses such as cheese-making and preserving, while others let guests help out with the *vendemmia* (grape harvest).

10 BASILICA DI SAN FRANCESCO

Dominating the landscape, Assisi's basilica *(p108)* is a beacon for pilgrims and art lovers alike. Inside, admire the frescoes depicting the life of St Francis, Italy's patron saint.

11 ANCIENT RUINS

Umbria's human history stretches back thousands of years. Ancient sights dot the landscape, from prehistoric settlements to Etruscan ruins and Roman remains.

12 ORVIETO'S UNDERGROUND WONDERS

Lying below Orvieto's streets is a vast, centuries-old underground network of caves, wells and cisterns. Explore this subterranean world on a tour with Orvieto Underground *(p125)*.

EXPLORE
UMBRIA

This guide divides Umbria into 3 colour-coded sightseeing areas, as shown on the map below. Find out more about each area on the following pages.

Pieve Santo Stefano

Mercantello sul Metáuro

Sansepolcro

San Giustino

Fraccano

Città di Castello

Morra

Trestina

Montone

Castiglion Fiorentinó

Camporeggiano

Umbertide

Monteroni d'Arbia

Sinalunga

Lisciano Niccone

NORTHERN UMBRIA *p60*

Riccio

Passignano sul Trasimeno

Lago Trasimeno

Magione

Colle Umberto I

Castiglione del Lago

Perugia

TUSCANY

Mugnano

Fiume Nestore

Chiusi

Panicale

Torgiano

Castiglione d'Orcia

Piegaro

Deruta

Città della Pieve

Montegabbione

Marsciano

Radicofani

San Casciano dei Bagni

Fabro Scalo

Pantalla

Santa Fiora

Ficulle

San Venanzo

UMBRIA

Roccalbegna

Prodo

Todi

Acquapendente

Orvieto

Castel Giorgio

Baschi

Sorano

Guardea

Pitigliano

Lago di Bolsena

Alviano

Manciano

Amelia

Farnese

Marta

Capalbio

Grotte Santo Stefano

LAZIO

Nera

Soriano nel Cimino

Magliano Sabina

0 kilometres 15
0 miles 15

N ↑

Monte Romano

Ronciglione

Montalto di Castro

Civita Castellana

Fossombrone

Senigallia

Acqualagna

Ostra

Pergola

Iesi

Pietralunga

Cantiano

Sassoferrato

Apiro

Filottrano

Scheggia

Gubbio

Sigillo

Fabriano

Villa Potenza

Mengara

Branca

Gualdo Tadino

Matelica

San Severino
Marche

Tolentino

Bosco

Valfábbrica

Castelraimondo

Mogliano

Ponte
San Giovanni

Assisi

Nocera
Umbra

Caldarola

Bettona

Valtopina

Muccia

MARCHE

**CENTRAL
UMBRIA**
p98

Spello

Foligno

Bevagna

Casenove
Serrone

Visso

Amandola

Montefalco

Sellano

Preci

Montemonaco

Bastardo

Trevi

Castel
Ritaldi

Campello
sul Clitunno

Triponzo

Castelluccio
di Norcia

Massa
Martana

Nera

Norcia

Acquasanta
Terme

Spoleto

Scheggino

Logna

**SOUTHERN
UMBRIA**
p144

Acquasparta

Cascia

Montecastrilli

Monteleone di
Spoleto

Strettura

Ferentillo

San Gemini

Arrone

Terni

Narni

Piediluco

Poggio
Bustone

Calvi
dell'Umbria

Rieti

Montenero
Sabino

LOCATOR MAP

SWITZ.

HUNGARY

FRANCE

ITALY

CROATIA

SERBIA

UMBRIA

ALBANIA

GREECE

ALGERIA

TUNISIA

*Mediterranean
Sea*

GETTING TO KNOW
UMBRIA

Snuggly sitting within the geographical heart of Italy, Umbria is best known for its pastoral landscapes and fortified medieval towns. Yet this landlocked region has much more to offer, including rugged mountains, such as the Apennines, and sparkling lakes, like Lago Trasimeno.

PAGE 60

NORTHERN UMBRIA

The north of the region is home to Umbria's capital, Perugia, a medieval city with a cosmopolitan vibe that's known for its summertime jazz festival, big student population and amazing art gallery, the Galleria Nazionale dell'Umbria. Other historic towns are scattered across the hilly emerald-green landscape, from fortified Gubbio to pretty Città della Pieve. To the west of the region sits Lago Trasimeno, a vast, island-sprinkled body of water, while to the east lie the lofty peaks and subterranean cave systems of the Parco Regionale del Monte Cucco.

Best for
World-class art and architecture, outdoor adventures

Home to
Città di Castello, Parco Regionale del Monte Cucco, Gubbio, Lago Trasimeno, Perugia

Experience
Take to the water in a rowing boat on Lago Trasimeno

CENTRAL UMBRIA

Covering two broad valleys, Central Umbria's gently undulating terrain is a patchwork of farmland, vineyards and olive groves. Pockets of hills coated by dense forests are a forager's paradise, with porcini mushrooms and black truffles waiting to be discovered. The region is also known for its hilltop towns, including Spello, Todi and Assisi, with the latter – home to the magnificent Basilica di San Francesco – the region's crown jewel. Elsewhere lie the famous springs of Fonti del Clitunno and the wooded hills and winding rivers of the Parco Fluviale del Tevere.

Best for
Local food and drink, medieval towns

Home to
Assisi, Parco Regionale del Monte Subasio, Spello, Todi, Orvieto

Experience
Strolling around the cobbled streets of medieval Orvieto

SOUTHERN UMBRIA

This lesser-visited part of Umbria is a mix of pastoral valleys and forest-clad hills, plus two parks: the mountainous Parco Nazionale dei Monti Sibillini and the Parco Fluviale del Nera. Southern Umbria is also home to a smattering of charming towns, such as Amelia and Norcia, as well as larger cities, including hillside Spoleto and Terni. Among other highlights are the ruined Roman settlement at Carsulae, to the west, and the wildflower-filled plains beneath the hilltop hamlet of Castelluccio di Norcia, found to the east.

Best for
Hiking, festivals, wildflowers

Home to
Parco Nazionale dei Monti Sibillini, Spoleto, Terni, Parco Fluviale del Nera

Experience
The splendour of the wildflowers blooming at Castelluccio di Norcia

←

1 View from the leafy Giardini Carducci.

2 Frescoes in the Collegio del Cambio.

3 Exhibit at the Galleria Nazionale dell'Umbria.

4 Piazza IV Novembre and Palazzo dei Priori.

Umbria spills over with travel possibilities, from days exploring hilltop towns to longer trips through bucolic countryside. Wherever you choose to go, our handpicked itineraries will help you plan the perfect trip through Italy's green heart.

24 HOURS
in Perugia

▌ *Morning*

Start your exploration of Umbria's capital at the Museo Archeologico Nazionale dell'Umbria *(p78)*. Housed in an old monastery, this spot displays Etruscan and Roman archaeological finds that provide a glimpse into the earliest days of the city; highlights include a display of bronze chariots from the 6th century BCE. Once you've had your fill of ancient artifacts, wander up to the Porta Marzia, a beautifully carved Etruscan archway that was incorporated into the imposing Rocco Paolino fortress *(p78)* in the mid-16th century. From here head up to the Giardini Carducci, a pretty park set atop the mighty fort. This green oasis offers stunning views across the city to the fields and hills beyond. In need of a pick-me-up? Chocolate shop Negozio Perugina *(p81)* is just a hop, skip and jump away, where you can enjoy some of Perugia's famous bite-sized *baci* chocolates – they're delicious.

▌ *Afternoon*

When you're ready for lunch, amble over to La Bottega di Perugia *(p81)*. This diminutive sandwich shop might be small, but it serves up hefty paninis. Take yours to-go in a brown paper bag and make for the Piazza IV Novembre, found in the medieval heart of the city. Here, perch up alongside the city's students on the steps in front of the Duomo *(p80)* and enjoy your lunch with a view of the Fontana Maggiore *(p84)*, one of the most important Romanesque monuments in Italy. The square is also watched over by the Palazzo dei Priori *(p84)*, a 13th-century Gothic palace and your next stop. Inside lies the Galleria Nazionale dell'Umbria *(p86)*, a world-class art museum that's filled with a truly impressive collection of Umbrian masterpieces, from the Renaissance to the modern age. Spend a couple of hours perusing the artworks, then make a beeline for the Collegio del Cambio (also found within the Palazzo dei Priori). There are three rooms to explore, but if you're short on time go straight to the Sala dell'Udienza (Audience Hall) to admire the stunning frescoes by Perugino – and see if you can spot the artist's self-portrait at the base of a vault.

▌ *Evening*

As the sun starts to descend, potter on over to Bottega del Vino *(p82)*, a welcoming *enoteca* overlooking Piazza IV Novembre; it's the perfect place for a well-deserved *aperitivo* and a spot of people-watching. Dinner at Il Giurista *(Via Bartolo 30)* is next on the menu. This cosy spot, located on a charming, stair-stepped lane, serves up moreish platefuls of homemade pasta. End the evening with a bitter Amaro *(digestivo)* or thimble-sized limoncello.

→

1 Hilltop Rocca Maggiore.

2 Looking towards the Temple of Minerva.

3 Frescoes inside the Basilica di San Francesco.

4 Lavender products outside Il Lavandeto di Assisi.

2 DAYS
in Assisi

Day 1

Morning There's no better way to get to know Assisi than by visiting the impressive basilica dedicated to its most famous son and Italy's patron saint, St Francis *(p108)*. Dominating the west of the city, the Basilica di San Francesco *(p108)* is a popular sight thanks to the eye-catching frescoes that decorate its interior – aim to get there early to beat the crowds. There's so much to see in the basilica that it'd be easy to spend the whole day here, but tear yourself away for a late lunch at Bar San Francesco *(Via San Francesco 52)*. Situated across the street from the basilica, this homely spot offers dishes like crispy artichoke hearts, saffron and truffle risotto, and veal *osso buco* with porcini mushrooms.

Afternoon After lunch, take a stroll east through Assisi's historic centre towards the Piazza del Comune, pausing to grab gelato at the Gelateria Artigianale *(Via San Francesco)*. The narrow lanes surrounding the square are sprinkled with shops: top picks include Il Lavandeto di Assisi *(p107)*, a cute little store selling products made with local lavender, and Tipografia Libreria Zubboli *(p107)*, a stationery shop filled with things like handcrafted artisanal paper and beautiful leather notebooks.

Evening As the sun sets, enjoy an *aperitivo* and some authentic Umbrian snacks at Enoteca Mazzini *(p104)*, a local wine bar stocking an incredible variety of vintages. Just a two-minute walk away lies tonight's dinner spot: Osteria Piazzetta dell'Erba *(p104)*. This cosy restaurant is one of the only places in Assisi that offers outdoor seating.

Day 2

Morning Enjoy a leisurely breakfast of a cappuccino and pastry at Bar Sensi *(Corso Mazzini 14)*, a local favourite just down the street from the Piazza del Comune. Nearby lie more sights linked to St Francis, including the Cathedral San Rufino, the city's Duomo *(p102)* where the saint was baptized, and the church of Santa Chiara *(p102)*, which is dedicated to St Clare, a devout follower of St Francis. Spend the morning exploring both sights; the latter is home to the San Damiano Crucifix, whose depiction of Jesus was said to have spoken to St Francis. Nearby, on Piazza San Rufino, is Da Andrea, a tiny *pizza taglio* (pizza-by-the-slice), with benches where you can enjoy a fresh slice.

Afternoon It's not far from here to the Temple of Minerva *(p103)*. Erected during the 1st century BCE, the building was once an ancient Roman temple – a fact attested to by the Corinthian columns that mark its façade – but its interior was transformed into a Baroque church. The visual contrast of these two periods of history is striking. Back out in the daylight, climb up to the Rocca Maggiore *(p105)*, a well-preserved 14th-century feudal fortification. From the top, you'll have awe-inspiring views of the Basilica di San Francesco and the surrounding valley below.

Evening Treat yourself to a night of fine-dining at La Locanda del Cardinale *(p104)*, whose glass floor provides views of the ruins of a Roman *domus*. Afterwards, amble towards the Wine Assisi Tesori dell'Umbria *(p104)*, a welcoming spot overlooking the basilica, for a glass of wine and, if you're still peckish, a cheeseboard.

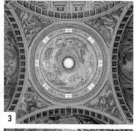

←

1 Castiglione del Lago.

2 Palazzo dei Consoli in Gubbio.

3 Città di Castello's Duomo.

4 A path in the Parco Regionale del Monte Cucco.

5 DAYS
in Northern Umbria

Day 1: Perugia

Spend the day in Perugia, starting with San Domenico *(p79)*, a huge church just off Corso Cavour; its stained glass is stunning. After an hour or so, stroll towards La Moglie Ubriaca *(Via Alessi 30)* in the city centre, a charming spot that serves up home-style cooking. Next, wander the serpentine streets of the Porta Sole quarter to visit San Severo *(p82)* and stop off at the Palazzo Bourbon-Sorbello for its 3rd-century BCE Etruscan Well *(p81)*. It's been a busy day, so end it with a delicious plate of handmade pasta at Osteria a Priori *(www.osteriaapriori.it)*.

Day 2: Lago Trasimeno

Take an hour-long train ride from Perugia to Castiglione del Lago, a town perched on the shores of the vast Lago Trasimeno *(p76)*. Spend a couple of hours touring the 16th-century Palazzo della Corgna before enjoying lunch and a glass of wine at lake-side Osteria Nova *(www.osterianova.it)*. After, hire a bike from Cicli Marinelli Ferrettini *(www.trasimenobike.eu)* and pedal along a section of the 50-km (31-mile) cycle path that skirts the shoreline. As the sun sinks below the lake, have dinner at Ristorante L'Acquario *(www.ristorantelacquario.it)* before jumping on the train back to Perugia.

Day 3: Città di Castello

Hire a car and set off for historic Città di Castello *(p64)*. The city's 11th-century Duomo, with its carved wooden choir and little museum, makes for a great first stop, while the nearby Torre Civica – a medieval tower that offers incredible views of the city – is another must. After lunch at La Piazzetta *(p65)*, take a 20-minute walk or bus ride to Collezione Burri Ex Seccatoi del Tabacco *(p67)*, which houses a display of monumental works by contemporary artist and Umbrian local, Alberto Burri.

Day 4: Gubbio

Drive south to charming Gubbio *(p70)*, which is dotted with Roman ruins, Gothic churches and Renaissance architecture. With so much to see, focus on the sights in the medieval quarter, such as the Palazzo dei Consoli *(p74)* which houses the town's civic museum; highlights include the famed Eugubine Tablets, a series of ancient bronze slabs. It's not far to the Palazzo Ducale *(p70)*, where you can enjoy a light lunch in its gardens at Il Giardini Pensili *(p72)*. After, make your way to the Teatro Romano *(p70)*. This impressive Roman theatre, built in the 1st century CE, has well-preserved arches and a number of excavated mosaics. As evening arrives, reward yourself with a refreshing Aperol spritz on the panoramic terrace of the Hotel Relais Ducale *(www.relaisducale.com)*.

Day 5: Parco Regionale del Monte Cucco

Grab a coffee and stock up on snacks at Al Ponte *(Via dei Consoli 16)*. You're going to need them: today will be spent exploring the wildlife-filled Parco Regionale del Monte Cucco *(p68)*. Start off at the Grotta di Monte Cucco, an impressive network of caverns and caves that lie underneath the park. Ascending back into the light, it's time to break out those snacks you packed earlier. Then, fully fuelled, hike one of the trails that crisscross the park – you could even tackle the summit of Monte Cucco. After all that adventuring, feast on traditional Umbrian grub at cosy Albergo Monte Cucco "Da Tobia" *(www.albergomontecucco.it/en)*.

1 Assisi's impressive Basilica di San Francesco.

2 Orvieto Underground.

3 A pottery shop in Deruta.

4 Festivities in front of Todi's Gothic Duomo.

5 DAYS
in Central Umbria

Day 1: Orvieto

Start your five-day road trip around Central Umbria in Orvieto (*p124*). After a lazy breakfast at Bar Da Brozzi (*Via del Duomo 27*), head to the magnificent Duomo (*p130*). Gaze in awe at its striking façade, complete with intricate bas-reliefs and a sublime rose window, then step inside to admire its beautiful interior, including stunning frescoes. Next, it's time for a filling lunch of fresh pasta at rustic La Palomba (*p129*), before journeying beneath the city on a tour with Orvieto Underground (*p125*); here, you'll get to explore a subterranean maze of caves and wells, built by the Etruscans centuries ago. After, spend some time ambling around the city's medieval streets, before enjoying a pizza in the garden of Charlie (*p129*).

Day 2: Parco Fluviale del Tevere

After breakfast at Palace Caffè (*Piazza del Popolo 24*), drive east to the Parco Fluviale del Tevere (*p132*), a protected natural park with countless outdoor adventure options, including kayaking and rock climbing. Fancy a walk? Experienced hikers can tackle the Gole di Prodo, a deep gorge that's home to a number of birds of prey. For a gentler option, head to the village of Titignano to tackle the footpath that loops through scenic cypress groves. As evening descends, jump back in your car and head to hilltop Todi (*p120*) to spend the night.

Day 3: Todi

At the heart of the town is Piazza del Popolo, home to the Gothic Duomo (*p121*). Admire its impressive works of art before heading to Gran Caffè Todi (*p123*) for lunch.

Spend the rest of the afternoon wandering Todi's hilly streets, perhaps popping into the museum found inside the impressive Palazzo del Capitano (*p120*) to learn about Todi's long history. Cap off the day with dinner at Vineria San Fortunato (*p123*).

Day 4: Deruta

Roll into pretty Deruta (*p135*) for some pottery shopping. A hub for Umbria's majolica ceramic production, the town's historic centre is dotted with countless artisan workshops. Once you've filled your bags, make for the Museo Regionale della Ceramica, which has over 6,000 works that highlight the importance of ceramics to the town. Lunch is at Osteria Il Borghetto (*Via Borgo Garibaldi 102*), an intimate restaurant offering dishes like *tagliatelle con il tartufo*. Back in your car, make for Assisi, pausing at Madonna dei Bagni along the way; this beautiful church is decorated with Deruta-made pottery.

Day 5: Assisi

The most important sight in the rosy-stoned town of Assisi (*p102*) is the Basilica di San Francesco (*p108*), which houses the final resting place of St Francis. A short distance away is the medieval quarter, where you'll find Mangia.Bevi.Ama (*Via San Francesco 20*), a perfect spot for lunch. After, climb the steep stairway of Sant'Andrea to reach the Piazza di Santa Margherita, which offers incredible views back towards the basilica. Wander back through the town centre to the Museo and Foro Romano (*p104*) to gaze at Roman finds, including the remains of an old piazza. End your trip at Trattoria Spadini (*Via Sant'Agnese 6*) with a plate of truffle *strangozzi*.

→

1 Castelluccio di Norcia's blooming wildflowers.

2 Marmore Falls.

3 Piazza San Benedetto in Norcia.

4 One of Terni's pretty streets.

3 DAYS
in Southern Umbria

Day 1: Terni

Begin your Southern Umbrian adventure in Terni *(p156)*. A great place to start is the church of San Francesco *(p158)* with its outstanding fresco cycle of *The Last Judgment*. Not far from here is Zero Zero Bakery Cafè *(Via Cavour 72)*, where you can pick up a couple of slices of freshly made pizza for a picnic. Wind your way along Terni's streets, stopping to admire the beautiful exterior of the 11th-century church of Sant'Alò *(p156)*, before reaching the Anfiteatro Romano *(p156)*. Spend an hour or so admiring these well-preserved Roman ruins, then nip into next-door La Passeggiata. This leafy garden is the perfect place to kick back and eat your pizza. From here, head across the river to the Centro Arti Opificio SIRI (CAOS) *(p158)*. This gallery houses an impressive number of contemporary works, including pieces by Mirò, Picasso and up-and-coming artists. End your day back in the centre at Urban Beer House *(p158)* for a burger with an Italian twist (think pesto and buffalo mozzarella) and a beer.

Day 2: Parco Fluviale del Nera

Drive or take the bus from Terni to reach the Parco Fluviale del Nera *(p160)*, just east of the city. This leafy park is famous for the Marmore Falls, a cascading waterfall that was built by the Romans in the 3rd century BCE. Note the falls aren't always flowing, so check the schedule beforehand on the park's website. One of the best places to see this thundering torrent of water is at the Belvedere Superiore viewpoint, where, if you're lucky, you might even spot rainbows arcing across the water. Afterwards,

take a stroll along one of the park's paths: those wanting an easy amble can follow the route to the Belvedere Inferiore viewpoint for more great vistas across the falls, while those wanting a tougher challenge can follow the Ferentillo path, a trail that switchbacks to the church of Santo Stefano. Ready to move on? Make a beeline for Norcia *(p162)*, where you'll spend the night – just make sure to enjoy a Michelin-starred dinner at Ristorante Vespasia *(p163)* before you turn in (make sure to book ahead).

Day 3: Norcia

After breakfast, wander into Norcia's historic centre through the Porta Romana (Roman Gate), arriving at the main square and heart of the town, Piazza San Benedetto. This plaza is surrounded by piquant *norcerias* (butchery shops) selling all manner of local cured meats, cheeses and the most famous of fungi: *tartufo nero* (black truffle). Spend some time tasting a bit of everything and then pick up some delicacies to take home. Afterwards, make the 40-minute drive to Castelluccio di Norcia, on the edge of the Parco Nazionale dei Monti Sibillini *(p148)*. Still showing deep scars from the earthquake that struck almost a decade ago, the winding streets of this pretty hilltop village are nevertheless a delight to stroll through. Plus, if visiting during late spring to early summer, you might get to see an explosion of wildflowers – including cornflowers and wild mustard – blanketing the large plain beneath the village. The spectacular natural display is a wonderful way to end your tour of Southern Umbria.

Cook Up a Storm

Want to learn how to rustle up delicious Umbrian dishes? Get tutored by a local cook. One of the best is Allerona-based chef Simona Fabrizio, who offers cookery classes in a traditional farmhouse *(www.sagraincasa.com)*. Many of the ingredients come from her own garden, including eggs from her chickens. Or why not head to Cantine Goretti, near Montefalco, for a class with Italian grandmother Nonna Marcella *(www.vinigoretti.com/en/cooking-class)*? She'll help you master the art of homemade pasta and *torta* (cake). Plus, after class you can enjoy the fruits of your labour, washed down with a glass of Sagrantino wine.

$\rightarrow$

Cooking up delicious Italian cuisine at a class offered by Simona Fabrizio

UMBRIA FOR
FOODIES

Umbrian food might be regarded as rustic and uncomplicated, but that doesn't mean that it skimps on flavour. In fact, the region is known for many delicious dishes, from truffle-covered pasta to fragrant roasted pork, all of which are made with fresh, seasonal and locally sourced ingredients.

Say Cheese

Umbrians adore cheese, whether it's tangy pecorino grated over asparagus or creamy ricotta mixed into pasta. Smooth *capra* (goat's cheese) is another local favourite; stop by Fattoria Il Secondo Altopiano *(www.ilsecondoaltopiano.com)* to sample this turned-by-hand cheese and meet the goats who helped create it. At Montelupo Farms *(www.fattoriamontelupo.com)*, meanwhile, learn how velvety *mozzarella di bufala* is made using traditional methods.

$\leftarrow$

Shelves lined with pungent goat's cheese, a local favourite

Market days

Many towns and villages hold regular market days, where stalls are piled high with local produce. Those in Todi *(p120)* and Orvieto *(p124)* offer some of the best farm-to-table pickings, with everything from fresh fruit and vege-tables to the region's famed truffles up for grabs.

→

A market stall in Orvieto laden with fruit and vegetables

Meaty Delights

Game and cured meats are big in Umbria. For the latter, head to Norcia *(p162)*, which is famed for its varied options, including salty-yet-sweet *prosciutto* and *cojoni di mulo*. Don't miss sampling the region's beloved *torta al testo umbra* (fried bread stuffed with salumi, sausage or porchetta).

→

A slice of delicious *torta al testo umbra*, a local speciality

THE FLAVOURS OF UMBRIA

Like their Etruscan ancestors, Umbrians have an affinity with the land and enjoy hunting for edible bounty from the countryside. As such, there's an earthiness to the region's cuisine and a real focus on what's in season. In spring expect wild asparagus, and in summer fruit and herbs. Autumn and winter have their fair share of culinary delights; as the weather turns colder, game, such as hare and pheasant, appear on market stalls and restaurant menus, and chestnuts, porcini mushrooms and truffles are readily foraged.

LENTILS

The plains of Castelluccio di Norcia, at the foot of the Monti Sibillini, are famous for the production of lentils, a pest-resistant, protein-rich legume that's grown using only organic methods. The lentils are awarded an IGT certification, which means only products grown in the area can be called Lenticchia di Castelluccio di Norcia. Ever versatile, they're used as a base for soups; cooked with sausage and vegetables into a hearty stew; or served as a cold salad, often in combination with farro, a spelt-like grain that also grows in Umbria.

TRUFFLES

Truffles, porcini mushrooms, chestnuts and wild asparagus are among the most

↑ A selection of freshly foraged truffles on display

→ A *salumeria* (delicatessen) in Norcia selling a wide range of cured meats

SLOW FOOD SANCTUARY

Founded in Italy in 1989, the now-global Slow Food Movement works to preserve local food cultures and traditions, and cultivate public interest in sourcing quality food. In Umbria, the organization has 17 different chapters, which organize local food events, promote sustainable farming, and advocate for small food purveyors, growers and restaurants that prioritize locally sourced, quality products.

commonly foraged foods in Umbria. Truffles are especially coveted, with *tartufaie* (truffle hunters) taking their highly trained dogs into the woods to nose them out. These pungent fungi are then shaved over pasta, eggs or meat dishes. Black truffles are more common, and can be found from spring to autumn in Umbria. Winter white truffles have an extremely strong flavour and are much more expensive than black truffles, being rarer and more perishable.

CHEESE
A variety of cheese is produced in Umbria, using milk from cows, sheep, goats and even water buffalo. *Cacio* is a mild cheese made from cow or sheep's milk, while pecorino is an aged sheep's cheese similar to parmesan and sometimes flavoured with truffles or *pepperoncini* (hot chilli peppers). Ricotta, meanwhile, is a mild sheep's cheese, often used for filled pastas like ravioli, or eaten with a drizzle of honey. Several small-scale farms also produce goat's cheese, mozzarella and buffalo mozzarella; the latter is made from the milk of Italian water buffaloes.

SALUMI
Umbria is famous for cured meats and charcuterie, which have traditionally been valued for their long shelf life. One of the most popular is *prosciutto crudo*, thin slices of salted, dried pork, which are enjoyed in the summer alongside melon as *prosciutto con melone*. Other varieties of dried, aged pork include *capocollo* (a cut of pork neck) and *culatello* (pork thigh). Salami is also a regular item on menus, and may be flavoured with locally sourced fennel, truffles and other spices. The cured meats from the hilltop town of Norcia *(p162)* are especially prized.

TOP 4 UMBRIAN DISHES

Tegamaccio
This stew from Lago Trasimeno includes fish like perch and trout in a tomato-and-wine broth.

Cinghiale alla cacciatore
Wild boar cooked with red wine, herbs and vegetables until tender.

Lenticchia di Castelluccio di Norcia
Umbria's famous lentils are often served as an accompaniment to fennel pork sausages.

Strangozzi
This pasta is served with sugar, walnuts, cinnamon, cocoa and lemon on Christmas Eve.

Medieval Towns

Umbrians began building fortified hilltowns during medieval times to protect against invaders; in the process they created some of the area's most beautiful settlements. Admire the mighty walls of Assisi (p102), impregnable fortresses such as the Rocca Albornoziana (p152) or simply wander through Orvieto's medieval quarter.

The medieval hilltop town of Assisi, surrounded by green peaks

UMBRIA FOR
HISTORY BUFFS

Thanks to a rich and lengthy history, almost every corner of Umbria is dotted with some sort of nod to the region's past. Here, uncover Etruscan necropoli, admire early Roman settlements and explore the medieval castles and fortresses, all left behind centuries ago.

ETRUSCAN INNOVATION

While much about the Etuscans is shrouded in mystery, we know that they were adept at civil engineering. Along with constructing wells, they used hydraulic technology to build dams, agricultural irrigation systems and *cuniculi* (water channels). They influenced the Romans, too, by showing them how to use survey instruments to build their famous roads. This advanced civilization was also proficient at winemaking and producing terracotta pottery.

→

An Etruscan necropolis in Orvieto, one of several found in the city

Umbri and Etruscan Ruins

Evidence of the Etruscans (p55) can be found across Umbria, from Perugia's ingenious Etruscan Well (p81) to necropoli and cave systems in Orvieto (p124). The Umbri (p55) may have left a less distinctive mark, but their influence can still be felt at Gubbio's Palazzo dei Consoli (p74), home to the Eugubine Tables, bronze tablets that describe things like religious rites.

↑ The impressive remains of Gubbio's 1st-century BCE Teatro Romano

Roman Remains

Markers of Umbria's time under Roman rule *(p55)* still dot the region, with Roman ruins found in towns such as Gubbio *(p70)*, which is home to the well-preserved Teatro Romano, and Spello, with its splendid Villa dei Mosaici *(p116)*. Other highlights include once-powerful Roman towns, such as 2nd-century CE Ocriculum *(www.otricoliturismo.it/parco-archeologico)* and Augustan-era Carsulae *(p168)*. Visit the latter to admire the Cura and Gemini temples, which overlook a largely intact forum.

💬 INSIDER TIP
Tread Lightly

Ancient ruins are fragile and irreplaceable, so it's important to treat archaeological sites with respect. Always stay in designated areas, avoid touching the ruins and never remove artifacts.

Prehistoric Sights

Umbria was first inhabited in the Neolithic period, with modern-day towns like Deruta established during this time. Finds from both this era and later periods, such as the Bronze Age, can be seen at the Museo Archeologico Nazionale dell'Umbria *(p78)*, including tools, weapons and ceramics. Go even further back in time at Foresta Fossile di Dunarobba *(p169)*, which is home to the three-million-year-old trunks of fossilized trees.

The Museo Archeologico Nazionale dell'Umbria and ↑ *(inset)* a Bronze-Age disc

ARCHITECTURE IN UMBRIA

Umbria is best known for its beautiful fortified hilltowns, which were built during the Middle Ages and the Renaissance period by a mixture of feudal lords and papal rulers who were determined to exert control over this bucolic region. Monuments from all periods of history are found dotted across the rolling landscape, though. From the time of the Umbrian and Etruscan city states to the era of Roman domination, from the rise of Romanesque architecture to the arrival of Post-Modernist styles, every people, every era, every architectural style and every artistic movement has left evidence of its existence, thanks to the efforts of the major artists of each period.

The Piazza IV Novembre, with the Duomo to the left ↑

The chambers were placed according to the terrain.

Architrave, often bearing the deceased's name

Walls in local stone

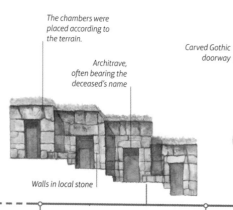

Pointed arched windows

Carved Gothic doorway

Architectural Styles

Antiquity

△ While the Umbri left few traces, the imposing polygonal walls of Amelia and Spoleto owe their existence to this Italic people. Scant evidence remains of the wattle-and-daub houses of their contemporaries, the Etruscans; however, examples of this group's necropoli _(above)_, such as Orvieto's Necropoli del Crocifisso del Tufo _(p128)_, still stand. The Romans, with their use of stone, marble and cement, left much more extensive material remains, including the Temple of Minerva in Assisi _(p103)_, the theatre in Gubbio _(p70)_ and old towns such as Carsulae _(p168)_ on the Via Flaminia, which still links Rome with the Adriatic coast, as it did 2,300 years ago.

Romanesque and Gothic

△ Around 1000 CE, Umbrian architecture was rejuvenated by the birth of the Romanesque, a style distinguished by its thick walls, round arches, groin vaults and small windows. A mix of religious and public buildings were erected in this vein over the next few centuries, with Assisi's Santa Maria Maggiore _(p106)_ an excellent example. During the 14th century, the advent of the Gothic style saw new buildings constructed with pointed arches, soaring ribbed vaults and ornate façades and windows. Two especially fine examples of this style are found in Perugia: the city's Duomo _(above)_ and the Palazzo dei Priori _(p84)_.

TOP 3 MEDIEVAL FORTRESSES

Rocca Maggiore
This 12th-century fortress in Assisi (p105) was rebuilt in 1356 on the foundations of a feudal fortification.

Fortezza dell'Albornoz
Begun in 1364 and then rebuilt in 1450, this fort (p128) in Orvieto was once surrounded by a moat and drawbridges.

Rocca Albornoziana
Spoleto's 14th-century, rectangular fort (p152) has four watchtowers.

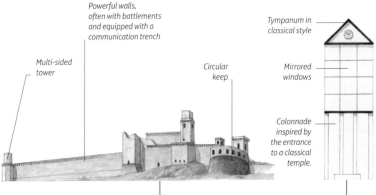

Multi-sided tower

Powerful walls, often with battlements and equipped with a communication trench

Circular keep

Tympanum in classical style

Mirrored windows

Colonnade inspired by the entrance to a classical temple.

Fortified Hilltop Towns

△ Hilltop towns are one of Umbria's defining architectural features. The period of their construction, called the *incastellamento*, began in the early Middle Ages, following the fall of Rome when local communities relied on feudal lords for protection. This led to the latter constructing walled fortifications around towns such as Spello (p114). The papacy took control of Umbria in the 12th century, and then extended its military control in the 14th century. It did this by either commissioning new fortresses or updating old ones, such as the Rocca Maggiore (above). These structures often had high, crenellated battlements and imposing watchtowers.

Modern Architecture

△ Outside the encircling walls of Umbria's medieval towns, large and small, modern suburbs have developed, usually on the flat land just below the hilltop towns. The new buildings that have been erected have not always complemented the artistic beauty of the old towns. However, there are some successful examples of modern architecture, such as the quarter of Fontivegge in Perugia (p78). This area was built by the architect Aldo Rossi between 1982 and 1989 in a Post-Modern style, featuring buildings that are both futuristic and full of classical references. Among the most eye-catching is the Palazzo della Regione (above).

Majestic Mountains

Umbria is blessed with epic mountain scenery, thanks to the Apennine range running down its eastern edge. These mountains are home to several national parks, each with their own impressive peaks. For panoramic alpine views, visit the Parco Nazionale dei Monti Sibillini *(p148)* to climb the soaring Monte Vettore. Want mountain views without the effort? The summit of Monte Cucco *(p68)* can be reached by car. All you need to do is park up and take in the vista of folded green mountains stretching out below.

→

Looking up at one of the Parco Nazionale dei Monti Sibillini's many peaks

UMBRIA FOR
NATURAL
WONDERS

There's more to Umbria than its rolling green hills, however beautiful they are. With everything from mountain peaks to flower-sprinkled plains, there's a wealth of incredible landscapes for visitors to get out and explore.

Flower-filled Plains

From late spring to early summer, the plains of Castelluccio di Norcia are transformed by La Fiorita *(p148)*, a display of blooming wildflowers that grow naturally among the town's famed lentil crops. The Altopiano di Colfiorito *(p140)* also sees wildflowers sweep across its plains, while the fragrant lavender fields outside of Assisi *(p102)* draw the eye with their purple hue.

←

A blooming lavender field, one of many located near to Assisi

UMBRIAN WILDLIFE

Umbria's varied land-
scapes underpin a
range of ecological
networks, which in
turn support a large
number of species.
Birds are particularly
prolific here, with the
likes of owls, partridges
and kingfishers calling
the region home; golden
eagles and peregrine
falcons have also been
seen here. Mammals
include porcupines,
wildcats, badgers and
weasels, as well as
apex predators, such as
grey wolves and lynx,
which roam Umbria's
more remote areas.

Subterranean Marvels

The region's subterranean scenery is just
as impressive as its above-ground offer-
ings. For an underground adventure,
visit the Parco Regionale del Monte
Cucco (p68), home to a vast network
of caves, grottoes and caverns. Other
sights include the Cave of Chiocchio
near Spoleto (p150) and the holy caves
in the Parco Regionale del Monte Subasio
(p112), where St Francis (p108) would pray.

← Exploring the subterranean wonders
found in the Cave of Chiocchio

Watery Oases

This bucolic region has a
boundless supply of picturesque bodies of water. Make
time to visit one of the lakes:
two of the most popular
are the vast island-dotted
Lago Trasimeno (p76) and
the glistening blue-green
waters of secluded Lago di
Piediluco. Want to glimpse
the immense power of water?
Go on a scenic trek to
Marmore Falls in the Parco
Fluviale del Nera (p160) –
this powerful cascade will
take your breath away.

→ Taking in the thundering
flow of Marmore Falls in
the Parco Fluviale del Nera

UMBRIA
RAISE A GLASS

Much like its northern neighbour Tuscany, Umbria is known for its incredible wine, sourced from the many vineyards that lie sprinkled across the region. Yet there are many more tipples to discover here, including monk-brewed beers and delicious dessert wines.

Dessert Wines

Umbrians round off their meals with a sweet dessert wine, such as the boozy Vin Santo or ruby red Montefalco Sagrantino Passito. Head to Lungarotti *(www.lungarotti. it/eng/vinsanto)* to sample the former, while the Enologica Montefalco wine festival *(p52)* offers tastings of the latter. Overindulged? Orvietan is the answer. Grab a bottle of this herb-infused *digestivo*, which is claimed to soothe stomachs, at L'Orvietan Amaro Erboristico *(www. lorvietan.com)* in Orvieto.

Grapes being stored at Lungarotti, ready to be made into wine

Visit the Vines

Winemaking is a time-honoured tradition in Umbria, so there are many vineyards to explore. One of the best is Tili Vini *(www.tilivini.com/ en/wine-tasting)*, where you can take a guided tour of the organic vineyard and cellar, then sample a selection of the wines alongside local eats. If you want to relax among the vines, book into the Wine Chalet at Roccafiore Wine Resort & Spa *(www.roccafiore. it)*, a pretty spot encircled by leafy vineyards and silvery olive groves; it also offers tours and tastings.

Sampling the wine on offer at Roccafiore Wine Resort & Spa

Beer Scene

Entrepreneurial brewers have set up microbreweries across Umbria, with places like Don Navarro *(www. lasostanavarra.it)* in Gubbio and FE3.Ø *(p129)* in Orvieto offering some great options. For award-winning brews, try those by Birra Nursia *(www. birranursia.com)*, a brewery run by Benedictine monks - the dark, malty "Extra" is delicious.

Bottles of Birra Nursia, brewed by monks in a monastery outside of Norcia

Wine To-Go

Practised in Umbria for centuries, *vino sfuso* (essentially wine on tap) was a way for winemakers to off-load surplus inventory. Grab a clean, reusable container and visit the likes of Sapori di Vino in Terni *(Via Narni 198/b)*, one of the many *enotecas* which continue the tradition. As the wine is so fresh, it's better sipped sooner rather than later - "cin cin!".

↑ An Umbrian *enoteca*, one of many that offer *vino sfuso*

▽ Climbing Courses

The Parco Fluviale del Nera *(p160)* is best known for its waterfall, but it's also home to excellent rock climbing. First-timer climber? Numerous schools operate out of Montefranco, a small village in the park, taking newbies on trips up manageable cliff faces. Experts should head to the Parco Regionale del Monte Cucco *(p68)* to tackle narrow Forra di Riofreddo, the park's most striking gorge.

△ Equine Adventures

Explore the beauty of the region from the saddle. Poggiovalle *(www.poggiovalle.com)* has courses to help you hone your horsemanship skills, as well as excursions with professional guides. La Somma *(www.lasomma.com)*, meanwhile, will take you on tours through chestnut groves and beautiful alpine meadows.

UMBRIA FOR
OUTDOOR ACTIVITIES

Like your holidays active? Umbria has you covered. There are countless activities on offer here, including canoeing, cycling and climbing – all of which take place in the region's beautiful outdoors.

△ Wonderful Walks

Umbria is a walker's dream, with lots of trails crisscrossing the region. Those after an easy amble can follow the riverside, waterfall-dotted path from Pian d'Assino to Serra Partucci near Umbertide *(p90)*. For a tougher hike, loop around Lago di Pilato in the Parco Nazionale dei Monti Sibillini *(p148)*, an alpine lake encircled by mountains.

▽ Cycling Circuits

There are cycling options aplenty here, including shoreside cycling around Lago Trasimeno *(p76)* and mountain biking in the likes of Monte Cucco *(p68)* and Monte Subasio *(p112)* regional parks. The route between Assisi and Spoleto *(p142)*, meanwhile, takes you through typical Umbrian scenery, passing by sheep-dotted fields and pretty hilltop villages.

△ Take to the Water

There's no shortage of options for water babies in this lake-dotted and river-laced region. Make a beeline for lakes Trasimeno *(p76)* or Piediluco, where you can glide across the water's silky surface in a kayak, canoe or sailing boat. For those looking for an adrenaline rush, another option is to head to the Parco Fluviale del Nera *(p160)* to brave the rushing waters of the Nera River in a rubber raft, canoe or kayak.

▽ Perfect Powder

While it doesn't offer as much downhill skiing as the Dolomites, Umbria still has options for speedy skiers in mountainous Parco Nazionale dei Monti Sibillini *(p148)*. Where it really excels, though, is in cross-country skiing, with the Centro Fondo Pian delle Macinare mountain resort in the Parco Regionale del Monte Cucco *(p68)* famed for excellent trails. Prefer stomping over sliding? This area also offers the chance to snowshoe through frosted beech forests.

Medieval Gatherings

Umbria's rich medieval past is celebrated in countless festivals. Many feature competitions, including flag throwing at Gualdo Tadino's Giochi delle Porte *(p52)* and crossbow shooting at Assisi's Festa del Calendimaggio *(p52)*. The biggest event is Bevagna's Il Mercato delle Gaite *(p52)*, where you'll encounter an array of becostumed jousters, jugglers and falconers.

Celebrations of medieval merrymaking at Il Mercato delle Gaite in Bevagna

UMBRIA FOR
FESTIVALS

Medieval re-enactments, colourful parades and energetic music performances: Umbria sure knows how to celebrate. Many of the region's festivals are deeply rooted in local culture and traditions and, no matter the season, you're sure to unearth an amazing event or two.

Flower Power

Beautiful blooms are the name of the game at Spello's L'Infiorata, a *primavera* (spring) festival that sees locals painstakingly decorate the streets with intricate designs made only from flower petals. The result is a staggering display of eye-catching colour and artistic talent *(p117)*. Other springtime extravaganzas include Castiglione del Lago's striking Festa del Tulipano (Tulip Festival) and the blooming of more than 600 beautiful rose plants in tiny Rocca Ripesena, known as the "town of roses".

Did You Know?
———
Around 2,000 people are involved in decorating the streets for Spello's L'Infiorata.

→

Local artists decorating Spello's streets with petals for L'Infiorata

Religious Celebrations

Umbria's cultural calendar is jam-packed with sacred events. Perugia's Festival of St Costanzo *(p52)* goes all out with lively parades, as does Orvieto's Feast of Corpus Domini, while the Festa dei Ceri in Gubbio draws thousands to witness the wild *ceri* (candlestick) race.

🔍 HIDDEN GEM
Carnival Time

Northern Umbria's San Leo di Bastia might be tiny, but it plays host to a truly vibrant parade on the first Sunday of carnival. Then, masked characters representing good and evil march through the streets.

← A parade during the Festa dei Ceri in the town of Gubbio

Performing Art Events

The sound of music is never far away here, with events including Città di Castello's celebration of classical tunes *(p53)* and Perugia's iconic Umbria Jazz, the region's biggest music event *(p53)*. Performances aren't limited to tunes, though: Baroque theatre takes place in Foligno *(p138)* and folklore dances in Castiglione del Lago *(p53)*, while a whole array of performing arts feature at Spoleto's Festival dei Due Mondi *(p53)*.

←

Performing live during the annual Umbria Jazz festival in Perugia

Foodie Feasts

There are plenty of food-focused festivals on the go here, including a celebration of Italian *primi* (first courses) in Foligno *(p52)*, chocolate in Perugia *(p52)* and black truffles in Norcia *(p52)*. Wash it down with the region's delicious wines: Spoleto hosts a three-day wine extravaganza in September *(p52)*, with the chance to taste local vintages.

→

Chocolate products on display at Perugia's Eurochocolate festival

Street Art

Colourful street art has popped up in cities across the region, with Terni leading the way. Explore the street art there via the Museo Aurelio De Felice's TAM (Terni Art Mapping) app, which leads visitors on an open-air art walk. Thanks to Street Art Umbria, there's plenty to find beyond Terni, including striking pieces near Perugia's train station and a timely depiction of a fish in a plastic bottle at Lago Trasimeno.

→

One of the pretty streets found in Perugia

UMBRIA FOR
ART

Umbria is bursting with art, whether it's Renaissance paintings hanging in world-famous museums or avant-garde street art decorating the walls of buildings. As you're sure to be inspired, Umbria also offers opportunities to get your own creative juices flowing.

Getting Creative

For those inspired by Umbria's artistic heritage, there are a number of creative classes to choose from, including photography lessons with Camera Etrusca *(www.cameraetrusca.com)* and pottery workshops at Scuola Internazione d'Arte Ceramica *(www.scuoladarteceramica.com/en)*. Want to channel Umbria's famous painters? Take a watercolour painting class in Orvieto *(www.kellymedford.com)*.

←

Caputuring the bucolic beauty of Umbria with Camera Etrusca

Curated Collections

Uncover centuries of art at Perugia's Galleria Nazionale dell'Umbria *(p86)*, with highlights including Renaissance masterpieces by Umbrian-born artists like Perugino. After more modern works? Head to the Centro Italiano Arte Contemporanea in Foligno for exhibitions by up-and-coming Italian artists.

→

A selection of the stunning works on diplay at the Galleria Nazionale dell'Umbria

Arts Festivals

Umbria plays host to several unique arty events. Civitella del Lago's decorative Easter egg competition *(p53)* sees elaborate designs painted onto eggs, while at Torgiano's arts and wine festival, I Vinarelli, local artists create paintings using tints diluted with wine.

←

A selection of painted eggs ready for Easter celebrations

TOP 4 RENAISSANCE PAINTERS IN UMBRIA

Luca Signorelli
This Renaissance master originally hailed from Tuscany.

Perugino
An Umbrian artist famous for his cycle of frescoes in the Collegio del Cambio *(p84)*.

Sister Plautilla Nelli
A self-taught artist, this nun was the first known female painter of the Renaissance *(p87)*.

Fra Filippo Lippi
This Carmelite priest painted grand cycles in Spoleto's Duomo *(p155)*.

Fabulous Frescoes

The Basilica di San Francesco *(p108)* contains some of Umbria's most stunning frescoes, depicting such things as the life of St Francis. But don't miss Luca Signorelli's superb *Last Judgment* in Orvieto's Duomo *(p130)* and the vibrant pieces by Pinturicchio in Spello's Santa Maria Maggiore *(p114)*, especially the detailed *Adoration of the Magi*.

↑ The striking frescoes found in Orvieto's Duomo

A Day on the Farm

Get out into the region's bucolic countryside with a trip to one of its farms. Family friendly Fattoria Didattica La Collina Incantata *(www.fattoria collinaincantata.com)* offers lots of activities for children, including tours of the farm and treasure hunts, as does Fattoria Il Bruco *(www. fattoriailbruco.com)*, with the chance for kids to get hands-on in the vegetable garden.

Picking fresh vegetables straight from the garden

UMBRIA FOR
FAMILIES

With family at its heart, Italy is the perfect place for kids – and Umbria is no exception. Children will be captivated by the region's science museums and farms, and will love letting off steam in its adventure parks. Plus, the sub-terranean sights are the perfect option for curious children and adults alike.

STAY

Il Fontanaro Organic Farm
Big holiday villas complete with a pool.

🅰B4 🏠Vocabolo Montanaro 64, Paciano 🖥countryslow living.com

€€€

Borgo Giorgione
Family-friendly resort offering fun day trips.

🅰B4 🏠Strada Provinciale 15, Monteleone d'Orvieto 🖥borgogiorgione.com

€€€

Going Underground

Exploring Umbria's many subterranean spaces is sure to be a hit with older kids. Uncover Narni's underground chambers at Sotterranea *(p164)* or tour Orvieto's labyrinth of caves, wells and rooms *(p125)*, made by the ancient Etruscans.

→

Exploring the underground rooms and passages beneath Orvieto

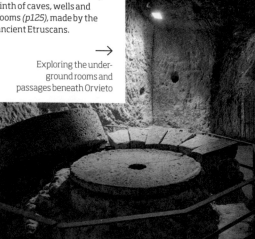

Fun On and In the Water

The region's lakes are perfect for a family day out, with Lago Trasimeno *(p76)* a great pick. The shoreline of this huge body of water is dotted with pretty beaches, such as Sualzo Beach, where kids can splash about in the water or build sandcastles. Then there's Parco Acquatico in Tavernelle *(www. azzurrapiscine.it/aquapark-tavernelle)*, a watery wonderland with slides for big children and a little lagoon for tiny tots.

↑ Families having fun on one of the beaches lining Lago Trasimeno

Hands-on Science Museums

Science-minded kids? Make for Spoleto's MuST, or Museum of Sciences and Territory, which provides ways for eager young minds to interact with geological specimens such as rocks and fossils *(www.intgeomod. com/must-3-2)*. Gubbio's EXTINCTION exhibition *(www.dinosauricarneossa.it/ gubbio)* is all about the history of life on the planet, with a special focus on big extinction events like that of the dinosaurs.

← One of the fascinating exhibitions found at MuST in Spoleto

Adventure Parks

Kids have excess energy? Take them to Umbria Activity Park and let them clamber through the trees on the junior adventure high-ropes course *(www. umbriactivitypark.it)*. The themed areas at Città della Domenica *(www.cittadella domenica.it)* are great for small children, and include a fairy-tale section complete with Snow White's house.

→ Children having fun on a high-ropes course in Umbria

Fashion Fix

Umbrian artisans have plenty to offer fashion-focused visitors. In Orvieto, master leatherworker Federico Badia *(www.federicobadiashoes. com)* handcrafts the likes of shoes, belts, purses and bags, while Perugia-based fashion brand Panicale *(www.panicale cashmere.com)* makes cashmere knitwear based on age-old techniques.

Rows of handmade shoes found outside an Umbrian shoeshop

UMBRIA FOR
LOCAL CRAFTS

Umbria has a long-standing history of crafting, something that can be seen in museums and historic buildings across the region. The region is home to countless creative crafters, many of whom use age-old techniques and traditions to create unique, handcrafted items.

Sublime Ceramics

Deruta *(p135)* is the undisputed hub of Umbrian earthenware. Explore the town's history of ceramics at the Museo Regionale della Ceramica or take a factory tour with one of the local makers such as FIMA Deruta *(www.fima deruta.it)*. In Orvieto, Ceramiche Fusari *(www.ceramichefusari. com)* is a great place to snag a *bocca di gallo* (green rooster pitcher) - it's one of the oldest dinnerware designs in Italy.

CRAFTING COURSES

Scuola Internazionale d'Arte Ceramica
🔲 scuoladarteceramica.com/en
At this Deruta institution, learn how to mould clay, spin a potter's wheel or paint a plate.

Giuditta Brozzetti
🔲 brozzetti.com/en/museum/weaving-courses
This Perugian museum offers summertime hand-weaving courses on a historic loom.

Scuola di Mosaico
🔲 shop.intessere.com/en
This Narni school shows students how to create Roman-style mosaics.

Wooden Wonders
Examples of Umbria's incredible woodwork are all around, from the Collegio del Cambio's exquisite stalls (p84) to the superb choir in Todi's Duomo (p121). To buy a modern-day masterpiece, visit Assisi's d'Olivo (www.dolivo.shop) or Orvieto's Bottega Michelangeli (Via Gualverio Michelangeli 3).

→
Crafting beautiful woodwork items at Bottega Michelangeli

Majestic Metalwork
Discover Etruscan-inspired jewellery at Oro degli Etruschi di Pettorossi Ulderico Giuseppe (Corso Vittorio Emanuele II 10), where expert goldsmiths repurpose the techniques practised by this early Umbrian group. Other metalwork experts are dotted across the region, including Spello blacksmith Luca Peppoloni (www.lofficina.net/en/tradizione), who creates hand-forged pieces that tell a story.

←
Some of the beautiful handmade items created by Luca Peppoloni

Artful Embroidery
Discover Umbria's textiles at the Museo del Tessile e del Costume (p153), which contains over 2,500 artful pieces. Learn the tricks of the trade with an embroidery course at the Museo del Ricamo e del Tessile (www.mostravaltopina.it) or visit Merletto (www.merlettodiorvieto.it) to purchase exquisite lacework.

→
An embroidered tablecloth, an example of Umbrian lacework

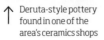

↑ Deruta-style pottery found in one of the area's ceramics shops

→
Participating in the
vendemmia
(grape harvest)

Harvest Time

Taking part in the *vendemmia* (grape) and *raccolta* (olive) harvests are a great way to get in tune with nature. From late summer to early autumn, many *agriturismos* in Umbria are happy to invite guests to take part. At Tenuta dei Mori (*www.tenutadeimori. com/en*) near Perugia, you can spend a day hand-picking grapes from the vines or shaking the branches of olive trees (the olives get caught by nets on the ground). After, reward yourself by sampling the farm's delicious wares.

UMBRIA FOR
SLOW TRAVEL

With its laid-back approach to life, Umbria is the perfect place for those looking for a more relaxed pace. Enjoy a meditative moment on a long walk, forage for food among glorious scenery or simply sit back and sip on a glass of wine in a Cittaslow - this region really knows how to live.

Mindful Moments

Umbria has lots of places that provoke peaceful contempla-tion, whether it's the tranquil waters of Lago Trasimeno *(p76)* or one of the region's serene churches. For a truly meditative experience, walk part of the Via di Francesco, dedicated to Italy's patron saint *(p108)*. One of the best sections is the Franciscan Path of Peace *(p94)*, which retraces the route taken by St Francis when he decided to abandon his life of comfort.

←

Contemplating the shimmering waters of Lago Trasimeno

← Kicking back with a drink in the main square of Montefalco, a Cittaslow

Laid-back Cittaslows

Umbria is dotted with a number of Cittaslows, community-focused cities that try to combat the stresses of modern life by promoting a slower, more considered way of living. There are many ways to experience this approach, including sipping on a glass of locally made wine in Montefalco *(p141)*, ambling around the medieval streets of Orvieto *(p124)* or sitting down to sample local produce in Trevi *(p140)* – all three are laid-back Cittaslows.

Did You Know?

In 2023, a record-breaking black truffle weighing 1.79 kg (3.9 lb) was found near Città di Castello.

Go Foraging

Umbrians love to spend time searching for nature's bounty in the region's pretty meadows and forests. Take a leaf out of their book and set off on a relaxed foraging trip with Reschio *(www.reschio. com/foraging)* to search for wild herbs and mushrooms. Or delve into woodlands on a tour with Tenuta San Pietro a Pettine to dig up some of Umbria's world-famous truffles *(www. sanpietroapettine.it/en)*.

↑ Truffle hunting with dogs and *(inset)* black truffles fresh from the ground

A YEAR IN
UMBRIA

JANUARY

La Fiera della Befana *(6 Jan)*. On Epiphany, the witch Befana flies (or rather, paraglides) from Monte Subasio into Rivortorto di Assisi, before handing out sweets to local children.

△ **Festival of St Costanzo** *(29 Jan)*. Perugia pays homage to its patron saint with a colourful parade.

FEBRUARY

△ **Festa di San Valentino** *(14 Feb)*. Betrothed couples exchange vows of love at the Basilica of St Valentine in Terni.

Sagra del Tartufo Nero *(late Feb)*. Tastings and sales of local produce, including cured meat and black truffles, in Norcia's main square.

MAY

△ **Festa del Calendimaggio** *(early May)*. This three-day medieval re-enactment in Assisi includes a crossbow shooting competition.

Corsa dei Ceri *(15 May)*. Three groups race to Gubbio's Basilica di Sant'Ubaldo carrying towering *ceri* (wax-covered wooden candlesticks) on their shoulders.

JUNE

△ **Mercato delle Gaite** *(late Jun)*. This historical re-enactment in Bevagna sees medieval markets, banquets and archery contests take place.

Festa delle Acque *(late Jun)*. A flurry of boat and canoe races, concerts and fireworks takes place on the shores of Lake Piediluco.

SEPTEMBER

△ **Enologica Montefalco** *(mid-Sep)* A three-day wine festival dedicated to the vintages of Montefalco and Spoleto, featuring tastings, workshops and cellar tours, and accompanied by food, music and art.

Giochi delle Porte *(last week Sep)* Dedicated to the Middle Ages, this festival in Gualdo Tadino includes flag-throwing and catapult competitions.

OCTOBER

I Primi d'Italia *(late Sep to early Oct)*. Foligno hosts this four-day food festival celebrating the *primi* (first courses) of Italian cuisine, including various types of pasta and gnocchi.

△ **Festival Eurochocolate** *(mid-Oct)*. Chocolate sculptures and stalls hawking sweet treats fill Perugia's historic centre.

APRIL

 **Coloriamo I Cieli** *(late Apr to early May)*. Lakeside Castiglione del Lago sees an array of colourful kites take to the skies for this biennial festival.

Mostra Concorso Ovo Pinto *(Easter Sunday)*. A long-standing Easter-egg-painting competition takes place in tiny Civitella del Lago.

Tableaux Vivants *(Holy Week)*. A week-long celebration in Città della Pieve, ending in costumed actors depicting scenes from the Passion of Christ.

MARCH

Trasimeno Ultramaratona *(early Mar)*. Thousands of runners participate in this 58-km (36-mile) annual ultramarathon, which loops around Lago Trasimeno.

△ **Estate Nursina** *(late Mar)*. Hundreds of locals from each *guaita* (quarter) of Norcia dress up in medieval costumes to celebrate the city's patron saint, Benedict.

AUGUST

△ **Rassegna Internazionale del Folklore** *(mid-Aug)*. Folk groups from Italy and across the world come to perform in lakeside Castiglione del Lago.

Festival delle Nazioni *(late Aug to early Sep)*. Città di Castello hosts this open-air, international event dedicated to chamber and classical music.

JULY

△ **Festival dei Due Mondi** *(late Jun to mid-Jul)*. Theatre, dance and music performances at Spoleto's iconic performing arts festival.

Umbria Jazz *(mid-Jul)* Perugia plays host to the world's greatest jazz musicians.

DECEMBER

△ **World's Largest Christmas Tree** *(early Dec to early Jan)*. Just outside of Gubbio, a giant Christmas tree illuminates the slopes of Monte Ingino.

Ri Fauni *(9 Dec)*. Norcia lights bonfires to illuminate the path of the angels who brought the Virgin's holy house from Nazareth to Loreto.

Presepe Vivente *(26 Dec)*. The citizens of Allerona put on an enchanting, living nativity scene throughout the hilltop village.

NOVEMBER

△ **Festa dell Olio Nuovo** *(early Nov)*. Trevi celebrates the olive harvest with tours of mills and tastings of newly pressed oils.

Feast of Santa Caterina *(25 Nov)*. Deruta's festival dedicated to the patron saint of ceramicists includes pottery exhibitions and workshops.

A BRIEF
HISTORY

With its central location and fertile soil, Umbria has long been a coveted region. The area changed hands many times throughout its history, whether between warring tribes, through Roman conquest or due to papal domination. Today, this Italian region celebrates its multifaceted heritage and traditions.

Early Peoples

The oldest evidence of human activity in Umbria dates to the Neolithic era, with traces of rock art in the region's east attesting to the existence of these early peoples. By the Middle Bronze Age, Umbria's inhabitants were cattle herders, setting up small, semi-permanent settlements in the Apennine Mountains. In the 12th century BCE, the Proto-Villanovans, a group originally from eastern Europe, had become predominant. Remains of their decorated funerary urns, jewellery and bronze armour indicate a hierarchical society with ritual practices.

Did you know?

Built by the Romans in the 3rd century BCE, Cascata delle Marmore is the world's largest artificial waterfall.

Timeline of events

8th century BCE
Etruscans establish the city of Velzna.

7th century BCE
Umbri found Tutere, modern-day Todi.

c 300 BCE
Romans found the town of Carsulae.

264 BCE
Roman conquest of Umbria is complete with the fall of Velzna.

Umbri and Etruscans

By the 9th century BCE, two highly advanced, often adversarial civilizations had emerged. Considered of Celtic-Gaulish origin, the Umbri dominated the region's east, while the Etruscans, believed to be descended from the Proto-Villanovans, controlled the west through a loose alliance of city states known as the Etruscan League. The Umbri founded modern-day Assisi, Terni, Spoleto and Todi, but little is known about their culture. The Etruscans left more extensive evidence of their society, including impressive necropoli in places like Orvieto.

The Rise of Rome

In the late 4th century BCE, the Romans arrived in search of trade opportunities and new lands. Alliances changed rapidly between the three groups, with both the Umbri and Etruscans at war or allied with Rome at different times. In 295 BCE the Romans defeated the Umbri and Etruscans, although some Etruscan city states held out for several decades. Velzna, modern-day Orvieto, was the last major city to be conquered by Rome in 264 BCE, cementing its domination of the region.

1 A historic map of the region of Umbria.

2 The carved exterior of an Etruscan sarcophagus.

3 A close-up of the Umbri's Eugubine Tablets.

4 The Roman army fighting Etruscan forces.

217 BCE
Roman army is defeated by Hannibal and the Carthaginians at Lago Trasimeno.

90 BCE
Umbri are granted Roman citizenship around this period.

219 BCE
Opening of the Via Flaminia, a trade route from Rome into Umbria.

1st century BCE
Romans build the Temple of Minerva in Assisi, one of many building erected during this time.

The Walled Hilltowns Go Up

After the fall of the Roman Empire in 476 CE, Umbria saw successive invasions by the likes of the Goths. This instability led to a period of *incastellamento*: the creation of fortified hilltowns, often controlled by noble families. Despite this, the Lombards managed to gain control of the area in the 6th century, setting up a dukedom known as the Duchy of Spoleto.

Later, in the 12th century, Rome's papacy established loose control of Umbria. Independent states (known as communes) still flourished during this time, however, and impressive buildings such as Perugia's Palazzo dei Priori were constructed.

The Renaissance

The Papal States gained full control of Umbria in the 14th century, and over the following centuries Umbria's cities became hubs of art and culture, largely thanks to the Renaissance. Mighty cathedrals and elaborate papal palaces were erected and decorated by important artists, such as Pietro Perugino. Agriculture thrived during this time, too, with the *mezzadria* (sharecropping system) introduced and the gradual colonization of the hills and plains.

1 A drawing of Narni, one of Umbria's hilltowns. ↑

2 One of the beautiful frescoes in the Basilica di San Francesco.

3 A battle that took place for the Risorgimento.

4 One of the pretty streets in medieval Assisi.

Timeline of events

6th century CE

The Lombards establish the Duchy of Spoleto.

1210

St Francis of Assisi founds the Franciscan Order.

1943

Terni, Foligno and other industrial cities are bombed by Allied forces.

1540

Pope Paul III suppresses a revolt in Perugia and builds the Rocca Paolina Fortress.

The Risorgimento and the Early 20th Century

In the mid-19th century, following the Risorgimento (a decades-long reunification movement), the Papal States were dissolved and the Kingdom of Italy was born, with Umbria becoming a province. The Industrial Revolution arrived in the region in the 1860s: a railway line linking Rome, Terni and Foligno was completed in 1866, and between 1875 and 1887 arms factories and the Terni steelworks were founded. However, most of Umbria's economy still relied on farming, especially olive oil and wine production.

Umbria Today

Following World War II, an economic boom fuelled the growth of many cities throughout Italy, including in Umbria. However, fortunes in many parts of the region were periodically affected by earthquakes, including major ones in 1979, 1997 and 2016. In the late 2000s, tourism began to take off in Umbria and today, this bucolic region now welcomes around 6 million tourists a year, drawn by the area's medieval hilltowns, incredible art museums, lively festivals and delicious cuisine.

ASSISI'S EARTHQUAKE

Due to its position above shifting tectonic plates, Umbria has a heightened risk of earthquakes. A violent one occurred in 1997, badly affecting Assisi, especially the Basilica di San Francesco, which saw parts of the vault in the Upper Church collapse. Through the hard work of restorers, fragments of frescoes were saved and rein-stalled where possible.

1970s

Umbrian farmers revive the near-extinct Sagrantino di Montefalco grape.

2022

The iconic Galleria Nazionale dell'Umbria reopens after an extensive refurbishment.

1973

The first Umbria Jazz festival takes place in Perugia.

2000

Assisi is recognized as a UNESCO World Heritage Site.

EXPERIENCE

Fishing on Lago di Piediluco

NORTHERN UMBRIA

While this region has been occupied since the Neolithic Age, little evidence of these first peoples remains. By the 12th century BCE, the area had become home to the Proto-Villanovans, a hierarchical society that had migrated here from eastern Europe. They settled on the west bank of the Tiber and, by roughly 900 BCE, had evolved into the Etruscans, an advanced civilization. This group vied for land and resources with the Umbri, another civilization who lived on the eastern side of the Tiber and about whom little is known. Over the following centuries, the Umbri established settlements like Gubbio and Città di Castello in the region, while the Etruscans set up cities such as Perugia.

The Romans arrived in the area around the late 4th century BCE, taking over Perugia in 310 BCE. Over the following centuries the area changed hands multiple times, falling under the control of Lombardy in the 6th century CE, followed by the Papal States in the 12th century. Different popes added their mark to the region's cities, including Pope Paul III, who built the imposing Rocca Paolina in Perugia during the 16th century.

In the 19th century, Northern Umbria, alongside the rest of the region, became part of the Italian Kingdom. Daily life changed little, however, with the area still heavily agricultural, something that remained true for most of the 20th century. Over the past several decades the tourism industry has developed, with many travellers coming to visit Perguia's world-class Galleria Nazionale dell'Umbria, take the waters in Nocera Umbra or explore the caves beneath the Parco Regionale del Monte Cucco.

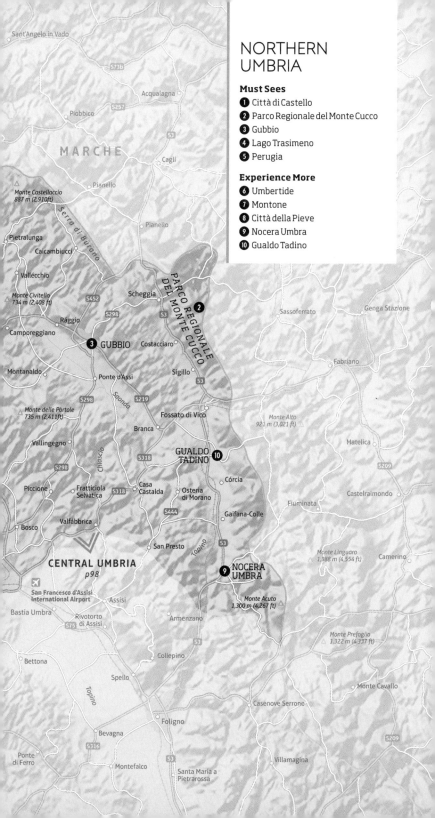

NORTHERN UMBRIA

Must Sees

1 Città di Castello
2 Parco Regionale del Monte Cucco
3 Gubbio
4 Lago Trasimeno
5 Perugia

Experience More

6 Umbertide
7 Montone
8 Città della Pieve
9 Nocera Umbra
10 Gualdo Tadino

❶

CITTÀ DI CASTELLO

🗺C1 🚗55 km (34 miles) NW of Perugia 🚆FCU Perugia-Sansepolcro line 🚌From Arezzo 🛈IAT Alta Valle del Tevere, Corso Cavour 5e; www.cittadicastelloturismo.it

Established by the ancient Umbri, this town grew in wealth during the Middle Ages, thanks to flourishing commercial activity. In the 16th century, it was completely redesigned under the Vitelli family, who built several stunning palazzi that can still be seen today. In the 20th century, industrial parks were erected, helping the town become the economic hub that it is today.

↑ Frescoes on the dome and choir above the Duomo's altar

①

Duomo

🏛Piazza Gabriotti 🕐Daily

It is immediately apparent that the cathedral exterior has undergone remodelling more than once. The round bell tower formed part of the original 11th-century building, but the body of the church reveals two successive rebuildings, in the 14th and the 15th–16th centuries. The unfinished Baroque façade dates from 1632–46. The interior has a single nave and contains a wooden choir and a *Resurrection* by Rosso Fiorentino (1529), in the chapel on the right-hand side. In the **Museo del Duomo**, objects on display map the evolution of the church in the Middle Ages.

Museo del Duomo

 🏛Piazza Gabriotti 3a 📞0758 554 705 🕐Apr-Sep: 10am-1pm & 3:30-6pm Tue-Sun; Oct-Mar: 10am-12:30pm & 3-5pm Tue-Sun

---

②

Palazzo Comunale

🏛Piazza Gabriotti 🕐Tower: closed for renovation until further notice

In the same piazza as the Duomo (typical of a medieval town) is the Palazzo Comunale, or town hall. This 14th-century

 HIDDEN GEM
Swan Park

Tucked outside the city walls on Via Vittorio Emanuele Orlando is this pretty little park. A path laces around a small pond, home to swans and other birds.

↑ The Duomo, amid a sea of red rooftops in Città di Castello

building is the work of Italian architect Angelo da Orvieto and shows how the Florentine influence on the town's architecture predates the arrival of the Vitelli family: in particular, the use of rusticated stone echoes the style of the Palazzo Vecchio in Florence.

In front of the palazzo, on the other side of the piazza, stands the Torre Civica, also built in the 14th century and once called "del Vescovo" (the bishop's), because it stood next to the bishop's palace (Palazzo Vescovile). From the top of the tower, there are good views over the town and the surrounding countryside.

---

③

San Francesco

⌂ Via Albizzini 20 ⊙ Daily

The street that cuts the city in half from north to south is made up of Via XX Settembre, Via Angeloni and Corso Vittorio Emanuele. Halfway along Via Angeloni, near the corner of Via Albizzini, is the church of St Francis, of 13th-century origin, to which the famous Florentine painter and architect Giorgio Vasari contributed in the 1500s. He was responsible for the Cappella Vitelli as well as an altar with a *Coronation of the Virgin* (1564).

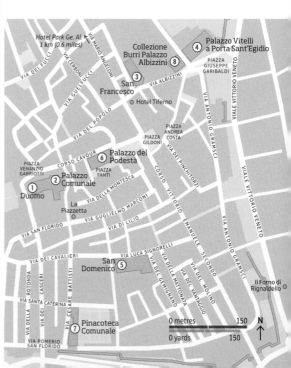

④

Palazzo Vitelli a Porta Sant'Egidio

 Piazza Garibaldi

A short distance from San Francesco is the splendid 16th-century Vitelli palace, one of many that the family had built in the town in an effort to impose some stylistic unity. The building's symmetrical façade features a grand porch; the original pillars were damaged in the 1789 earthquake and, as a result, were reconstructed into the larger pillars that can be seen today. Inside, a vaulted ceiling is decorated with frescoes by Italian painter Prospero Fontana, while the main hall is lined with paintings depicting the achievements of the Vitelli family.

In front of the palace is a pretty garden lined by oaks. At the far end of this space is Palazzina Vitelli, which was built around a medieval turret. Its loggia is decorated with more frescoes by Fontana, which depict landscapes and mythical scenes.

⑤

San Domenico

 Via G Muzi Betti 5D
 Daily

Between Piazza Garibaldi and the Pinacoteca is the church of San Domenico, the largest in the town. It was built by the Dominicans in the 15th century and later reworked, although the façade remains unfinished. Frescoes from the 15th century line the nave.

⑥

Palazzo del Podestà

 Corso Cavour

From the east of the piazza runs Corso Cavour, home to the Palazzo del Podestà. The façade facing the street dates from the same era as the Palazzo Comunale, and it may be that the original design was also by Angelo da Orvieto. The eastern

---

STAY

Hotel Tiferno
A former 17th-century monastery is now home to this boutique hotel.

 Piazza Raffaello Sanzio 13
Ⓦ hoteltiferno.it

€€€

Hotel Park Ge. Al.
This family-run hotel has a pool and a large tree-lined garden.

 Via Piero della Francesca 24
Ⓦ hotelparkgeal.it

€€€

←

The magnificent façade of the Palazzo del Podestà in Piazza Matteotti

side is Baroque and leads on to Piazza Matteotti, where the Palazzo Vitelli "in Piazza" stands.

Pinacoteca Comunale

🏠 Largo Monsignor G. Muzi
📞 0758 520 656 🕐 Apr–Oct: 10am–1pm & 2:30–6:30pm Tue–Sun; Nov–Mar: 10am–1pm & 3–6pm Tue–Sun

The Pinacoteca, one of the region's top art galleries, is housed in the Palazzo Vitelli alla Cannoniera, the most notable of the various Vitelli palazzi. It was built by Antonio da Sangallo (1521–32) with the assistance of Vasari, who was responsible for part of the frescoed friezes.

Among the many works are an *Enthroned Madonna and Child* by the Maestro di Città di Castello (early 14th century); a *Martyrdom of St Sebastian* by Luca Signorelli (1497–8); a *Gonfalone della Santissima*

Trinità by Raphael (1499); and a *Coronation of the Virgin* attributed to the workshop of Ghirlandaio (early 1500s). There is also a remarkable *Assumption of the Virgin* in terracotta from the workshop of Andrea della Robbia (early 16th century).

Collezione Burri Palazzo Albizzini

🏠 Via Albizzini 🕐 Hours vary, check website
🚫 Mon, 1 Jan, 25 Dec
🌐 fondazioneburri.org

Situated in a 15th-century palace, the Collezione Burri Palazzo Albizzini houses a range of paintings and sculptures by home-grown artist Alberto Burri. The 130 works on display date from 1948 to 1985, with many named after the materials they're made from, including Sacks, Metals and Cellotex.

The gallery has a sister site, the **Collezione Burri Ex Seccatoi del Tabacco**, on the outskirts of town. Housed in an enormous industrial-style complex, the gallery showcases some of

Burri's monumental pieces from the 1970s and 90s, and a nucleus of the artist's graphics work; there's also a documentary and photographic archive section. Collectively these exhibition spaces represent the most comprehensive assemblage of Burri's work on display anywhere in the world.

Collezione Burri Ex Seccatoi del Tabacco

🏠 Via Francesco Pierucci
🕐 Hours vary, check website
🚫 Mon, 1 Jan, 25 Dec
🌐 fondazioneburri.org

> 💬 INSIDER TIP
> **Say Cheese**
>
> Mozzarella fans should visit Fattoria Montelupo *(www.fattoriamonte lupo.com)*, the only farm in Umbria that makes creamy *mozzarella di bufala*. Tours include tastings and the chance to learn how buffalo milk is processed using ancient techniques.

←

Intricately decorated garden wall of the Palazzo Vitelli alla Cannoniera and *(inset)* the Pinacoteca, found inside the palazzo, displaying numerous artworks

→
Hang-gliding over the
Parco Regionale del
Monte Cucco

❷

PARCO REGIONALE DEL MONTE CUCCO

🅰 E2 🚗 37 km (23 miles) NE of the town of Gubbio 🚆 Fossato di Vico, Rome–Ancona line
ℹ Sede del Parco del Monte Cucco, Sigillo; www.parcodelmontecucco.it

Comprising green peaks and forested valleys, with the soaring Monte Cucco at its centre, the Parco Regionale del Monte Cucco is a paradise for outdoor lovers, who flock here to go hiking, climbing and caving.

On the border with the neighbouring region of Le Marche, this park stretches over more than 10,000 ha (24,700 acres). Its highest point is Monte Cucco, which sits 1,566m (5,136ft) above sea level, and is a popular summit for hikers. Through the park there are a number of other excellent hiking trails, as well as running tracts and mountain bike paths. Other adventurous pursuits include hang-gliding and caving; in fact, the park is home to one of the most impressive cave systems in Italy, the Grotta di Monte Cucco, which is made up of around 19 km (30 miles) of galleries and caverns. Expert climbers, meanwhile, can tackle the Forra di Riofreddo; this deep, narrow gorge was formed after many centuries of erosion by streams coming down from the mountaintop.

The park is also known for its pretty villages, several of which are of Roman origin. These include Scheggia, known for its Benedictine abbeys, like the Hermitage of San Girolamo a Pascelupo, and Scirca, with the fresco-adorned church of Santa Maria Assunta. The hilltop village of Costacciaro, however, is more medieval in style; it was was built in 1250 by the citizens of Gubbio as a fortified settlement.

> **The park is home to one of the most impressive cave systems in Italy, the Grotta di Monte Cucco, which is made up of around 19 km (30 miles) of galleries and caverns.**

STAY

Albergo Monte Cucco "Da Tobia"

This cosy mountain lodge is in a sunny, protected spot.

⌂ Loc Val di Ranco, Sigillo
🇼 albergomontecucco.it

€€€

La Piazzetta di Pascelupo

The rooms at this rustic bed-and-breakfast have mountain views.

⌂ Via Umberto Boccioni 1, Pascelupo
📞 3386 424 898

€€€

↑ Exploring one of the many caves found in the park

→
Costacciaro surrounded by the park's mighty peaks and wooded landscape

Monte Cucco's Wildlife

As well as outdoor activities, the Parco Regionale del Monte Cucco is one of the best places in the Apennines for observing wildlife. The park is home to typically Apennine species (such as deer, wild boar, porcupines and martens), but it also provides a habitat to other species that are becoming increasingly rare in central Italy, including the wolf and wildcat. Among the birds that can be seen in this park are partridges, quails, eagle owls and kingfishers; the area is also home to the golden eagle, another of central Italy's rarer species.

Did You Know?

Monte Cucco is made up of sedimentary rocks of marine origin, which date back to the Jurassic period.

GUBBIO

⚑ D2 ⚑ 40 km (25 miles) NE of Perugia 🚉 Fossato di Vico, 20 km (12 miles), Roma-Ancona line 🚌 *i* Via della Repubblica 15; www.comune.gubbio.pg.it

Founded by the Umbri, this town spread onto the plain, but after the Lombards invaded the people returned to the slopes, where they could defend themselves. In 1624, after coming under papal rule, Gubbio went through a long period of political and economic decline. Its fortunes revived, however, following the unification of Italy in 1860, and today it attracts visitors with its historic sights and striking architecture.

①

San Giovanni Battista

⚑ Piazza S Giovanni ⏰ Daily

From Piazza Quaranta Martiri, the steep Via della Repubblica leads to the base of the great structure supporting Piazza Grande *(p73)*. This is the entry point to the oldest part of the medieval city, where the first cathedral, dedicated to San Mariano, is believed to have stood. The site is now occupied by this church dedicated to St John the Baptist. The church, built in the 13th

and 14th centuries, has a Gothic façade with a Romanesque bell tower. The Gothic style continues inside, with characteristic coupled columns and great arches in stone.

②

Palazzo Ducale

⚑ Via Federico di Montefeltro 📞 0759 275 872 ⏰ 8:30am-7:15pm Tue-Sun (from 1:30pm Mon)

Locally known as the Corte Nuova, the restored Palazzo

HIDDEN GEM
Big Barrel

Near the Palazzo Ducale is the Botte dei Canonici, a huge wooden wine cask – accessed via the Martinelli Francesco souvenir shop – that dates from the Middle Ages and at the time was deemed the largest in Europe.

Ducale was built by the Montefeltro family. It has an archaeological area underground (featuring traces of the piazza that was here before the palazzo was built) as well as several rooms used for temporary exhibitions.

③

Roman Ruins

⚑ Via del Teatro Romano

The first Roman monument that you see as you arrive in Gubbio from the south is a mausoleum, a monumental tomb of which the burial chamber has survived with its barrel vault. Further on are the ruins of the Roman theatre

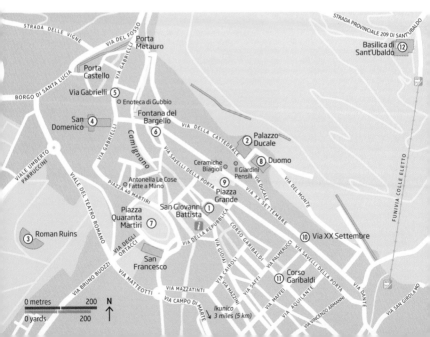

 The Roman theatre with Monte Ingino in the background

(Teatro Romano), which dates from the 1st century BCE. It accommodated around 6,000 spectators, and was faced in squared and rusticated blocks. Among other works uncovered are some beautiful mosaics.

---

④
San Domenico

🏛 Piazza G Bruno ⊙ Daily

At the heart of San Martino, in Piazza Bruno, is the church of San Domenico, which was built by the Dominicans in the 14th century on the site of a 12th-century church dedicated to San Martino. The interior was restored during the 18th century, but 16th-century frescoes from the Gubbio school remain; there is also a fine lectern decorated with inlaid wood.

---

⑤
Via Gabrielli

This street, lined with medieval houses, runs north from Piazza Bruno to Porta Metauro.

Near the end is the small but impressive Palazzo del Capitano del Popolo, whose façade curves in line with the road. Adorned with a series of small Gothic windows, the palazzo is a typical Gubbio construction from the late 13th century. Nearby is the park attached to the Palazzo Ranghiaschi Brancaleoni. Laid out in the mid-1800s, the garden extends south along the slopes of Monte Ingino as far as the Palazzo Ducale. There is a Neo-Classical temple here.

---

⑥
Fontana del Bargello

About halfway along Via dei Consoli, which connects the San Martino quarter and Piazza Grande, the street broadens out to form Largo del Bargello, the centre of the ancient quarter of San Giuliano. In front of the 14th-century palazzo of the same name – which houses the Gubbio Crossbow Society and museum – is this small yet charming fountain. Dating back to the 1500s but rebuilt in the 19th century, it is an excellent example of local Gothic architecture.

SHOP

Ceramiche Biagioli
Named after famed 15th-century ceramicist, Mastro Giorgio da Gubbio, this pretty shop sells traditional and contemporary pottery.

🏛 Piazza Grande 3
ⓦ ceramichebiagioli.com

Ikunico
Run by third-generation artisanal bookbinders, this store offers genuine vegetable-tanned leather goods and Fabriano acid-free paper.

🏛 Via Santa Maria Maddalena
ⓦ ikunico.com

Antonella Le Cose Fatte a Mano
This shop peddles everything from handmade sweaters to kitchen towels to wedding favours.

🏛 Piazza 40 Martiri 17
ⓦ antonellalecosefatte amano.it

DRINK

Enoteca di Gubbio

This is a wonderful place to sip local and seasonal vintages. There's also plenty of delicious natural wines.

📍 Via Nicola Vantaggi 11
📞 0759 274 780

Il Giardini Pensili

Soak up sunset views while enjoying a drink at this kiosk in the "hanging gardens" of the Palazzo Ducale.

📍 Via Federico da Montefeltro

---

⑦
Piazza Quaranta Martiri

This broad square is the principal point of arrival in Gubbio, as well as the best place to leave a car. It is dedicated to the 40 local people executed by the Germans in 1944 in an act of vengeance against the partisans. The lowest point in Gubbio, the piazza is a good place from which to gaze upwards to admire the full extent of the town.

Gubbio's finest church, San Francesco, dominates the piazza. Its construction was begun in the mid-1200s and continued at least until the end of that century (though the façade was never finished). Inside are three aisles without a transept. There is a fresco cycle by Ottaviano Nelli in the apse chapel on the left (*Scenes from the Life of Mary*, c 1408–13). The frescoes in the central apse, by an unknown artist, can be dated to around 1275, but they are badly damaged.

On the opposite side of the piazza is the Antico Ospedale (Old Hospital) of Santa Maria della Misericordia, a 14th-century building, with a long portico in front, surmounted by a loggia, added in the 17th century by the wool merchants' guild, which used the premises for some of its processing. Nearby stands the church of Santa Maria dei Laici, dating back to 1313 and now restored.

 Duomo's nave adorned with frescoes and a stained-glass window

⑧
Duomo

📍 Via Sant'Ubaldo 🕐 Daily

From Piazza Grande, Via Sant'Ubaldo climbs in a series of steps to the cathedral. This was founded in 1229 and enlarged around a century

↑ Piazza Quaranta Martiri, seen from the Palazzo dei Consoli's loggia

→

Spacious courtyard in the Basilica of Sant'Ubaldo

later. The façade has an entrance with an ogival arch and an oculus with bas-reliefs which belonged to the previous church on the site. Inside, the single nave is covered by a very high and distinctive stone "wagon vault", a local architectural speciality. There are many frescoes and other paintings, as well as some fine stained-glass windows.

Piazza Grande

Via dei Consoli follows the route of the old Umbrian fortifications before suddenly opening out into Piazza Grande. Quite apart from the importance of the buildings found here, the square is an extremely impressive piece of engineering: it is, in fact, an artificial space supported by walls and embankments.

In front of the more famous and much larger Palazzo dei Consoli *(p74)* is the Palazzo Pretorio (closed to the public), which was erected in the mid-14th century and designed by the same architect, Gattapone. On the last Sunday in May the traditional Palio della Balestra (a shooting competition involving the crossbowmen of Gubbio and Sansepolcro, over the border in Tuscany) takes place between the two buildings.

Via XX Settembre

From Piazza Grande, Via XX Settembre leads past palazzi and churches to the quarter of Sant'Andrea and the Porta Romana. This medieval town gate, with its high tower, houses a collection of majolica pottery and other pieces in various materials, as well as weaponry,

maps and so on. Nearby, outside the walls, is the church of Sant'Agostino, which retains traces of frescoes dating back to the church's foundation (1294), as well as several works dating from the 14th century.

A short walk east of the church is the terminal for the funicular up to the Basilica di Sant'Ubaldo, which lies high above the town on Monte Ingino. The ride takes 8 minutes and offers lovely views on the way; there is also a path, if you prefer to go up on foot.

Corso Garibaldi

This street runs parallel with the quarter of Sant'Andrea and is the main thoroughfare through the San Pietro quarter, the busy centre of Gubbio. The narrow streets retain a village atmosphere and are lined with shops. On Corso Garibaldi itself look out for the churches of Santissima Trinità and of San Pietro, of 13th-century origin and built close to a large monastery complex.

Basilica di Sant'Ubaldo

🏠 Via Monte Ingino 5
🕐 Daily

Perched atop Monte Ingino is the Basilica di Sant'Ubaldo, which takes its name from

Gubbio's cherished patron saint. Built on an existing medieval structure (work began in 1513), the building is mostly devoid of decoration on its exterior, giving it an imposing, almost fortified, feel.

Inside the church, above the main altar, the untouched body of the saint is visible inside a Neo-Gothic urn, surmounted by 20th-century stained-glass windows that beautifully recount his life. To the right, in the first of its five naves, are marble pedestals supporting massive, 10-m (33-ft) wax-covered wooden candlesticks. Known as *ceri*, they are used during the Corso Ceri di Gubbio (candle race) on 15 May, an event marking the anniversary of Sant'Ubaldo's death. On the evening of the festival, the *ceri*, bearing the effigies of Sant'Ubaldo, St George and St Anthony Abbot, are carried aloft over the 4-km (2.5-mile) course to the finish line at the basilica.

 GREAT VIEW
Funivia Colle Eletto

Ride the standing, aerial tramway Funivia Colle Eletto and soar from the city centre to the summit of Mount Ingino. From its cable cars, shaped like giant bird cages, you'll enjoy epic views over Gubbio and the countryside.

⑬ 🎨

PALAZZO DEI CONSOLI

🏛 **Piazza Grande** 📞 **0759 274 298** 🕐 **10am-1pm & 3-6pm daily (Nov-Mar: 10am-1pm & 2:30-5:30pm)** 🚫 **1 Jan, 13-15 May, 25 Dec**

Overlooking the Piazza Grande, this 14th-century palazzo, with a soaring bell tower and castle-like façade, is also home to two remarkable museums.

Designed by Angelo da Orvieto in 1332, this palazzo is supported by an impressive row of arched buttresses. The entrance, approached by a fan-shaped flight of steps, is a masterly example of the Gothic style. The palazzo houses the Museo Civico on the ground floor, which displays fragments of the Eugubine Tablets – seven bronze slabs that survived from the ancient city of Iguvium. They were engraved in the 2nd century BCE with text in the local language describing rites and sacred sites, and today provide crucial evidence of life in the region before the Roman conquest.

On the first floor, meanwhile, is the Pinacoteca Civica (art gallery). It houses a variety of works, including inlaid furniture from the 16th century and paintings by artists of the Umbrian School. There are excellent views of the town from the loggia.

The tower is crowned with battlements and has four apertures echoing the form of the windows below.

Illustration of the 14th-century Palazzo dei Consoli ↑

Arches, supporting the palazzo on the hill.

← The loggia that overlooks the town

VOICE OF GUBBIO

The "Campanone" or Great Bell in the palazzo's tower is called the "Voice of Gubbio" as it rings out during major events in the town, including the Festa dei Ceri. It weighs almost 2,000 kg (4,400 lb), with the clapper or "batocchio" alone weighing 114 kg (250 lb). A Latin inscription carved into the surface asks Jesus, Mary and the saints to free the town from the scourge of earthquakes, storms and other evils.

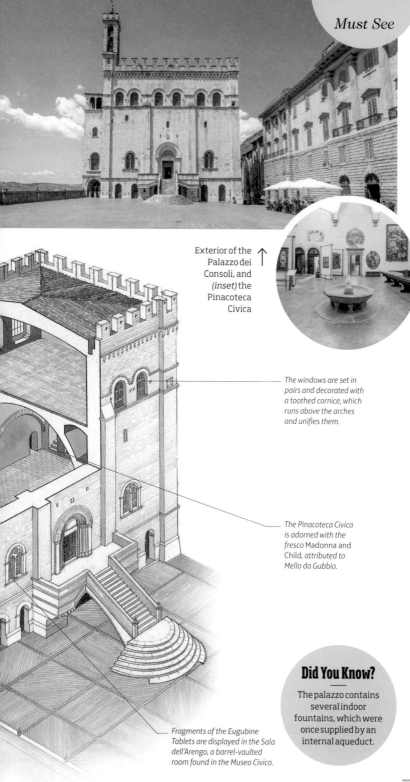

Exterior of the Palazzo dei Consoli, and *(inset)* the Pinacoteca Civica

The windows are set in pairs and decorated with a toothed cornice, which runs above the arches and unifies them.

The Pinacoteca Civica is adorned with the fresco *Madonna and Child, attributed to Mello da Gubbio.*

Fragments of the Eugubine Tablets are displayed in the Sala dell'Arengo, a barrel-vaulted room found in the Museo Civico.

Did You Know?

The palazzo contains several indoor fountains, which were once supplied by an internal aqueduct.

4

LAGO TRASIMENO

🅰B3 🚗 48 km (30 miles) NW of Perugia 🚌 🚐 🛈 Tuoro sul Trasimeno: Piazza Garibaldi 7, www.prolocotuorosultrasimeno.it; Magione: Corso Marchesi 24, 0758 43859; Passignano sul Trasimeno: Via Roma, www.italia.it

This vast, deep-blue lake near the border with Tuscany is nestled among rolling green hills and lined by a mix of oak woods, olive groves and medieval towns. Its tranquil atmosphere makes it the perfect place for a relaxing getaway.

Covering an area of 126 sq km (48 sq miles), Lago Trasimeno is the fourth-largest lake in Italy. Although the water levels rise and fall, and the lake periodically floods the surrounding land, the area has always been inhabited, and became important during the medieval period. The largest town is Castiglione del Lago, which occupies a promontory dominating the lake's western shore and is home to a number of interesting sights, including the 16th-century Palazzo della Corgna, the Rocca del Leone fortress and Neo-Classical Santa Maria Maddalena.

The lake offers a range of options for watersports enthusiasts, including sailing and windsurfing, while its shore has opportunities for walking and mountain biking with a 50-km (31-mile) cycling path around the lake.

Three islands, which are home to monasteries, convents and active fishing communities, dot the lake. Today, however, only Isola Polvese (the largest island) and Isola Maggiore are accessible to the public. The former, reached by ferry from the town of San Feliciano, has several small beaches that are great for wild swimming and a nature park with hiking trails that wind past ancient architectural marvels. Isola Maggiore, meanwhile, is known for its tiny fishing village, which has around 30 residents.

THE BATTLE OF LAGO TRASIMENO

After defeating the Romans at the battles of Ticino and Trebbia, Hannibal learned that Caius Flaminius was leading the Roman army towards Lago Trasimeno, and strategically positioned his soldiers in the hills on 21 June 217 BCE. Aided by foggy weather, he gave the order to attack the enemy forces. Trapped between the lake and the hills, the Roman soldiers suffered a crushing defeat.

Did You Know?

Lago Trasimeno is not only the largest body of water in Umbria, it's also Italy's largest non-Alpine lake.

① The tranquil Tuoro sul Trasimeno beach is perfect for families.

② Passignano, overlooking Lago Trasimeno, is one of the most beautiful villages in Italy.

③ Lago Trasimeno is an excellent spot for fishing.

←

Imposing medieval castle on a high summit overlooking Lago Trasimeno

5

PERUGIA

C3 27 km (17 miles) W of Assisi Cortona-Foligno & Rome-Perugia lines BusItalia: 0759 637 637 Piazza Matteotti 18; www.turismo.comune.perugia.it

Due to its strategic hilltop position, Perugia has long been coveted, with the Etruscans, Romans and papacy all controlling the city at one point. The largest city in Umbria, Perugia today has a distinctly cosmopolitan population and outlook, thanks partly to its large student population. The city also hosts many events, including Italy's top jazz festival, Umbria Jazz, and an annual chocolate festival, Eurochocolate.

① Rocca Paolina and Porta Marzia

Built in 1543, this fortress is a symbol of papal domination over Perugia. It was built on the orders of Pope Paul III Farnese, who sacked the city in 1540 and annexed it to the Church. Construction of the fortress was entrusted to Antonio da Sangallo, the best-known military architect of the age. Many other buildings were razed to make way for the Rocca. This only increased the hatred of the locals towards the edifice, which was destroyed as soon as the city gained independence from the pope in the mid-1800s. The gap created was filled with Piazza Italia.

Parts of the fortress survive, including the Porta Marzia, an Etruscan archway which Sangallo liked so much that he incorporated it into the wall of his own building. Beneath the archway is the entrance to the Via Baglioni Sotterranea, a medieval street once buried beneath the Rocca Paolina. Opposite the fortress, Giardini Carducci is a peaceful park dotted with trees and bronze busts. The garden offers panoramic views over Perugia.

②

Museo Archeologico Nazionale dell'Umbria

Piazza G Bruno 0755 727 141 8:30am-7:30pm Tue-Sun 3rd Sun of the month

Along Corso Cavour is the church of San Domenico and its attached monastery, now home to the Museo Archeologico. The collection reopened after a

> Built in 1543, Rocca Paolina is a symbol of papal domination over Perugia. It was built on the orders of Pope Paul III Farnese, who sacked the city in 1540 and annexed it to the Church.

major renovation in 2022 and there is now much more to see than the original Etruscan and Roman finds. The Carri Etruschi di Castel San Marino is a particularly fine exhibit of 6th-century BCE bronze chariots. Another must-see is the Cippus Perusinus, an Etruscan boundary stone that bears one of the longest inscriptions in Etruscan ever found.

③

San Domenico

🏠 Piazza G Bruno 📞 0755 724136 🕐 7am–noon, 4–7pm daily (tours by appt, call ahead)

This church was built in the 14th century, to a design reminiscent of the Florentine churches of Santa Croce and Santa Maria Novella. It was rebuilt in the Baroque style in the 17th century, but was never finished. Inside, the Cappella del Rosario has statues by Agostino di Duccio and a stained-glass window, the second largest in Italy after the one in Milan cathedral.

← Perugia's medieval centre, surrounded by distant hills

④

San Pietro

🏠 Borgo XX Giugno 74 📞 0753 3753 🕐 10am–1pm & 2–6pm Mon–Sat (summer: to 7pm)

Further along Via Cavour, beyond Porta San Pietro is one of the oldest religious buildings in Perugia, the Benedictine church of San Pietro. The church and abbey was founded in the 10th century, on top of an older 6th-century Christian building, which in turn was erected on the site of underground burial chambers used first by the Etruscans and then by the Romans.

Much of the original Romanesque church survives, including the partially frescoed façade. The decoration inside is late Renaissance, and includes cycles of large paintings reminiscent of those done by Tintoretto. There is also a painted coffered ceiling and wooden choir stalls, the work of various artists in the 16th century. The vault is frescoed with *Stories from the Old Testament*. In the sacristy are five small canvases by Perugino depicting the saints. Visitors need to ask the sacristan for permission to view the artworks.

💬 **INSIDER TIP**
Parking

If you're arriving in Perugia by car, it's best to leave your vehicle in the underground car park at Piazzale Partigiani. From here, you can hop on the escalator, which travels to the historic centre in around ten minutes.

⑤
Museo Capitolo

📍Piazza Danti ☎0755 723 832 🕐8:30am–12:30pm & 3:30–7:30pm Mon–Sat (Sun & public hols: to 7pm)

The Charter Museum, found next door to the city's Duomo, exhibits the cathedral's most important treasures. The displays follow a thematic route, linking artworks to the story of the Perugian territory. Among the items on display are the painting of the *Enthroned Madonna with Saints* (1484) by Luca Signorelli and a marble polyptych by Florentine sculptor, Agostino di Duccio. Other highlights include an ancient missal of songs for the liturgy and the Holy Ring, an ancient piece of agate suspended inside a gilded silver and copper reliquary, which dates from the 1st century CE. The latter is often referred to as the Virgin's "wedding ring", because it is believed to be associated with the marriage of Mary and Joseph.

⑥
Duomo

📍Piazza Danti ☎0755 723 832 🕐8:30am–12:30pm & 3:30–7:30pm Mon–Sat (Sun & public hols: to 7pm)

The Duomo, dedicated to San Lorenzo, was built on the site of a 10th-century basilica. The first stone was laid in 1345, but the Black Death delayed progress for many years, with work starting again properly in 1437.

Its façade is covered in pink and white marble, and features a Gothic doorway, designed by Galeazzo Alessi in 1568. In a niche above the doorway is a cross, beneath which the Perugians symbolically laid down the keys to the city following their defeat by Pope Paul III Farnese in the Salt War of 1540. In contrast, a statue of Pope Julius III, sculpted by Vincenzo Danti in 1555, was commissioned by the people of Perugia to celebrate the pope who had restored some communal liberty to the city. On the right is an unfinished, 15th-century pulpit, from which St Bernardino of Siena preached to vast crowds of Perugians in the 1420s.

On the side of the Duomo is Loggia Braccio Fortebracci, which was built in 1423 for Braccio Fortebraccio, the condottiere from Montone. The bare interior is reminiscent of northern European churches. Just past the entrance is the Cappella di San Bernardino da Siena, home to one of the two major works of art in the building, *Descent from the Cross* by Federico Barocci.

Underneath the cathedral is Underground Perugia, a series of ancient streets and buildings that can be explored on a 45-minute tour. The ruins include roads and structures built by the city's Etruscan, Roman and medieval-era papal occupants. Among the highlights are sacred buildings dedicated to the Etruscan goddess Uni (who later became the Roman Juno), the ruins of a Roman *domus* from the 1st century BCE and the "via delle cantine," where medieval clerics kept their food and drink.

The Duomo, together with the Loggia Braccio Fortebracci

Did You Know?

The Holy Ring, housed in the Museo Capitolo, is said to change colour according to who wears it.

The transept and main altar of the Duomo, and *(inset)* the staircase leading to its entrance

↑ Exploring the impressive remains of Perugia's ancient Etruscan Well

and Underground Perugia, forms part of the Isola San Lorenzo, a huge cultural complex, which also includes the excellent Museo del Capitolo.

---

 ⑦
Oratorio di San Bernardino

🏠 Piazza San Francesco al Prato 📞 0755 733 957
🕐 8am-12:30pm & 3:30-5:30pm daily

Heading down Via dei Priori, you cross what was once a main road through medieval Perugia. Beyond the city walls, the street widens into a piazza with the 13th-century church of San Francesco al Prato, which is now partially ruined. To the left of the church is the small 15th-century Oratorio di San Bernardino, whose fine bas-reliefs on the façade make it a masterpiece of the Umbrian Renaissance.

 HIDDEN GEM
Handcrafted Textiles

Close to the Oratorio di San Bernardino, the Museo Atelier Giuditta Brozzetti *(www. brozzetti.com)* is among the only surviving hand-weaving workshops in Italy. It displays original 18th-century looms and sells traditional prints.

Inside, in the first chapel on the left, is a 15th-century *gonfalon* (banner) showing the Madonna sheltering Perugia from the plague and the tomb of Braccio Fortebraccio da Montone. The altar was made from an ancient Early Christian sarcophagus.

---

⑧
Etruscan Well

🏠 Piazza Danti 18
🕐 10am- 2pm & 3-6pm daily (Aug: to 6:30pm)
🔒 1 Jan (am), 24 Dec (pm), 25 Dec 🌐 pozzo etrusco.it

The Etruscan Well (Pozzo Etrusco) in the basement of the striking Palazzo Bourbon-Sorbello, found next to the cathedral façade in Piazza Danti, is an astonishing feat of engineering. It was capable of providing a constant supply of water to the entire city. The well (the bottom of which is accessible) is partially covered in vast blocks of travertine, from which the original cover was also made. You can still see the furrows left by the ropes that were used to pull up the buckets of water.

Behind Piazza Danti is the district of Rione di Porta Sole, where the Rocca del Sole fortress was built in 1372. It was the largest fortification of its time, but was destroyed shortly after its completion.

Must See

EAT

La Bottega di Perugia
Try *porchetta* (roasted pork) panini here.

🏠 Piazza Francesco Morlacchi 4
📞 0755 732 965

€€€

Il Falchetto
Delicious Umbrian comfort food is served up in cosy surrounds.

🏠 Strada Fontana La Trinità 2/d
📞 0755 731 775

€€€

Pinseria Hamburgheria Torre Delgi Sciri
This joint is famous for its piled-high burgers.

🏠 Via dei Priori 96
📞 0755 723 029

€€€

SHOP

La Pianta del Tè
Choose from an amazing selection of coffees and teas.

🏠 Via dei Priori 2
🌐 lapiantadelte.it

Negozio Perugina
Browse the flagship of the city's iconic *baci* (kisses) chocolatier.

🏠 Corso Pietro Vannucci 101 🌐 negozioperugina. blogspot.com

Rastelli Play Store
This cute stationery store has a great selection of gifts for kids.

🏠 Corso Pietro Vannucci 63 🌐 rastellistore.com

DRINK

Punto di Vista
The splendid terrace at this cocktail spot offers some truly stunning city views.

🏠 Viale Indipendenza 2
📞 3338 432 929

Dempsey's
A favourite haunt with locals and students alike, this cool bar offers classic cocktails nightly.

🏠 Piazza Danti 19
📞 3318 113 524

Bottega del Vino
Drink wine by the glass or bottle at this characteristic *enoteca* overlooking Perugia's main drag.

🏠 Via del Sole 1
🌐 labottegadel vino.net

Kundera Caffé Bistrot
An ode to the speakeasy, Kundera has an excellent selection of wine.

🏠 Via Oberdan 23
📞 0753 725 435

Elfo Pub
This quirky dive bar, complete with a bicycle suspended from the ceiling, has over 15 beers on tap.

🏠 Via Sant'Agata 20
📞 3470 785 981

---

 ⑨

Piazza Matteotti
Running parallel to Corso Vannucci, this square is home to two notable 15th-century buildings. The first is the Palazzo del Capitano del Popolo, designed by Lombard architects Gasparino di Antonio and Leone di Matteo, and the seat of the judiciary in the era of the communes.

The palazzo was originally built on three floors, but the third was demolished following the earthquake of 1741. Behind the porticoes alongside the palazzo is a 1930s covered market, from where you can see the piazza foundations.

The other building of note is the Palazzo dell'Università Vecchia (Gasparino di Antonio collaborated in its construction, too); the building was made the seat of the university by Pope Sixtus IV in 1483.

---

 ⑩

Via dei Priori
Perugia's main road, Via dei Priori, is named after the Latin priori, referring to the ten magistrates who ran the city government from the Middle Ages until the beginning of the 18th century. This ancient artery was first built by the Etruscans and later became a Roman *decumanus* (an east-west-oriented road). It starts at the arch of the Palazzo dei Priori and continues slightly downhill, passing a mishmash of artisan workshops, tiny piazzas and sandwich

> **Via dei Priori is named after the Latin priori, referring to the ten magistrates who ran the city government from the Middle Ages until the beginning of the 18th century.**

shops along the way. Near the narrow lane's end is the monolithic symbol of the city, the Torre degli Sciri, a 42-m (138-ft) tower that is the last of around a dozen that once dotted the city in the Middle Ages. Inside, 232 steps lead to the roof, from where visitors can take in stunning views of the city. Just beyond the tower is the travertine-fronted Madonna della Luce church, with a small rose window adorned with festoons.

---

⑪

San Severo

🏠 Piazza Raffaello 📞 0759 477727 🕐 10am–6pm Tue–Sun 🚫 1 Jan, 25 Dec

The church of San Severo houses one of Raphael's earliest frescoes, the *Holy*

↑ Outdoor café on Piazza Matteotti, surrounded by historic buildings

Trinity and Saints. Perugino finished the work in 1521, adding the saints lower down on the same wall. Look out for the 16th-century terracotta group of a Madonna and Child by an unknown Tuscan sculptor. The church existed in the 11th century, but the site was probably used for sacred buildings before that. Its current appearance dates from the mid-18th century.

Arch of Augustus

⬛ Piazza Fortebraccio

A scenic descent signals the end of the Porta Sole quarter, marked by the 3rd-century BCE Arch of Augustus (Arco di Augusto). This civic gate is also known as the Etruscan Arch, since it was of Etruscan origin, and was later modified by the Romans. The still-legible inscription, "Augusta Perusia", was placed here by Octavius Caesar (later Emperor Augustus).

---

⑬

Borgo Sant'Angelo

Corso Garibaldi, running north from Piazza Fortebraccio, is the principal medieval street, along which the area of Borgo Sant'Angelo developed. Now the seat of Perugia's university, this district grew around an Augustinian monastery, and has the city's most important monastic buildings, including the monastery of San Benedetto, the former hospital of the Collegio della Mercanzia, the convent of Santa Caterina and the monastery of Beata Colomba

At the end of the road, in the shelter of the walls, is the circular church of **San Michele**

Arcangelo (Sant'Angelo), whose origins date back to the late 5th century. Thanks to excellent restoration work, major parts of the original church are now visible, along with a 14th-century Gothic doorway.

Around 7 km (4 miles) southeast of the city is one of the area's most interesting burial sites: the Ipogeo dei Volumni. It consists of a great tomb chamber where nobles of the Etruscan Velimna family were buried.

San Michele Arcangelo
⬛ Via del Tempio 📞 0755 722 624 🕐 9am–4pm daily

←

Façade of the 5th-century church of San Michele Arcangelo

(14) (M) (①)

PALAZZO DEI PRIORI

⌂ Corso Vannucci 19 ☎ Sala dei Notari: 0755 736 458 ⊙ All sights: hours vary, check website ☒ All sights: 1 Jan, 25 Dec ⓦ Palazzo dei Priori: www.gallerianazionaleumbria.it; Collegio della Mercanzia: www. mercanziaperugia.it; Collegio del Cambio: www.collegiodelcambio.it

This striking Gothic building is one of the most important in Perugia. Within its walls are four separate sights, including a historic art gallery.

Topped by crenellations, the Palazzo dei Priori was constructed in stages between 1293 and 1443. It is composed of several buildings, which in turn house four attractions: the Sala dei Notari, Collegio della Mercanzia and the Collegio del Cambio, plus the splendid Galleria Nazionale dell'Umbria (p86).

The Sala dei Notari, or lawyer's meeting hall, has magnificent vaulting and 13th-century frescoes painted by local artists. The Collegio della Mercanzia, meanwhile, was once a meeting place for merchants, and is adorned with rare 15th-century wooden panels. The Palazzo is also home to the Collegio del Cambio, where the city's moneychangers operated. It is made up of three rooms: the Sala dell'Udienza (Audience Hall), which is decorated with stunning frescoes by Perugino; the Sala dei Legisti, or Jurists' Hall, with its beautifully carved 17th-century wooden stalls; and the Cappella di San Giovanni Battista (Chapel of St John the Baptist), with more beautiful frescoes.

The Guild of Money Changers established its headquarters in the palazzo between 1452 and 1457.

The Collegio del Cambio houses a cycle of frescoes by Perugino, painted from 1496 to 1500.

On the ground floor, the walls of the Collegio della Mercanzia are lined with inlaid wood.

The Arco dei Priori marks the start of Via dei Priori, which, it is said, flowed with rivers of blood in the Middle Ages.

THE FONTANA MAGGIORE

Built from 1275 to 1278, this fountain is a feat of Italian architecture and hydraulic engineering. It has two poly-gonal basins, one in marble and one in bronze. Both feature bas-reliefs of episodes from the Old Testament, the Liberal Arts and the Labours of the Months, and sculptures of biblical and historical figures.

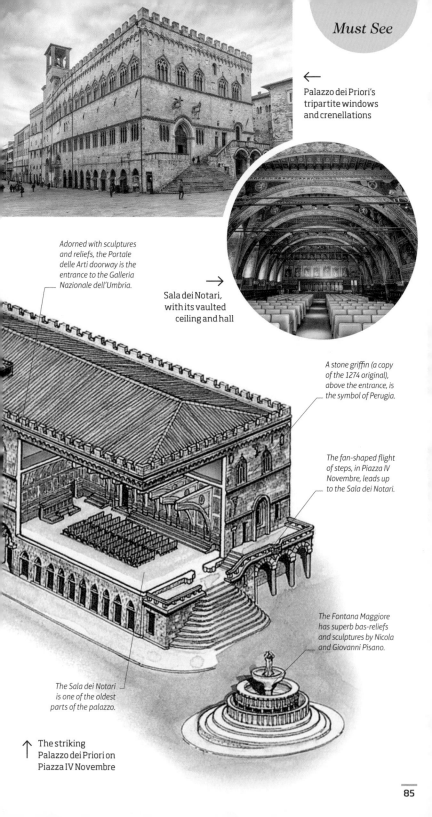

← Palazzo dei Priori's tripartite windows and crenellations

Adorned with sculptures and reliefs, the Portale delle Arti doorway is the entrance to the Galleria Nazionale dell'Umbria.

→ Sala dei Notari, with its vaulted ceiling and hall

A stone griffin (a copy of the 1274 original), above the entrance, is the symbol of Perugia.

The fan-shaped flight of steps, in Piazza IV Novembre, leads up to the Sala dei Notari.

The Fontana Maggiore has superb bas-reliefs and sculptures by Nicola and Giovanni Pisano.

The Sala dei Notari is one of the oldest parts of the palazzo.

↑ The striking Palazzo dei Priori on Piazza IV Novembre

Exploring the Galleria Nazionale dell'Umbria

This is the most important gallery, not only in Perugia but in the whole of Umbria, with works of art, largely Umbrian in origin, dating from the 13th to 19th centuries. Created partly out of Napoleon's seizure of artworks held by religious orders, the gallery was established in 1863. It was moved to the Palazzo dei Priori in 1879 and has been state-owned since 1918.

Renovation works in the early 2020s increased the amount of exhibition space at the gallery. Today, the impressive collection is spread over two floors and 40 rooms, including the 15th-century Cappella dei Priori, which features some splendid Perugian scenes. Around 500 pieces of art are on show, including paintings, textiles and ceramics, with items displayed chronologically. There's also the bookshop and the Sala Podiani, which hosts concerts and temporary exhibitions.

← *Madonna and Child Pentaptych* by Luca di Tommè at the gallery

> **Around 500 pieces of art are on show in the gallery, including paintings, textiles and ceramics, with items displayed chronologically.**

Some of the impressive artworks on display at the Galleria Nazionale dell'Umbria ↑

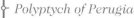

HIDDEN GEM
Ancient Relics

Hidden beneath the library of the Galleria Nazionale dell'Umbria is a room that's accessible only on request. Inside is a glass floor, underneath which lies the ancient remains of the city walls, dating to the Etruscan and Roman eras.

Museum Highlights

Polyptych of Perugia

Also known as the *Polyptych of St Anthony*, this work is an iconic masterpiece by Piero della Francesca. It took nearly 10 years to paint and was finally completed around 1470. This complex painting portrays the Virgin enthroned with the Child, flanked by the saints: Anthony of Padua and John the Baptist on the left, and Francis and Elizabeth of Hungary in the right. The centre is highlighted by a remarkable damask background that's been intricately painted in gold. The upper section shows the saints Claire and Lucy, while the lower part depicts stories of the main Franciscan saints.

Guidalotti Altarpiece

Originally painted by Beato ("Fra") Angelico (1395–1455) for the chapel of St Nicholas in Perugia's San Domenico *(p79)*, these two panels feature many tales of the saint's life and death against a dramatic backdrop of slender towers and far-off hills. The polyptych's panels were restored in their current arrangement in 1915, with rich gilded carpentry featuring late Gothic elements.

Adoration of the Magi

◄ Pietro di Cristoforo Vannucci (better known as Perugino) painted this oil panel in Perugia in 1504. The painting was originally commissioned for the city's church of Santa Maria dei Servi, but, in 1543, it was moved to the church of Santa Maria Nuova, also in Perugia. It depicts the Nativity scene with the Three Wise Men richly clad and offering gifts. To their right, the Virgin Mary is dressed in red and wearing a blue cloak. She holds the Infant Jesus to be blessed by the Magi as Joseph looks on.

St Catherine of Siena in the guise of Catherine de' Ricci

Born Pulissena Margherita in 1524, Sister Plautilla Nelli (a Dominican nun from Florence) painted this oil on canvas between 1560 and 1580. The painting was discovered by the museum when the monasteries were dissolved in 1810. The profound devotion of the saint to Jesus is mani-fested through the tears streaming down her face and the marks of the stigmata on her hands and chest.

The Painted Cross

▶ This monumental Crucifix, with St Francis kneeling at Christ's feet, was created for San Francesco al Prato in Perugia, but was moved in 1863 after the church's collapse. It was made by Maestro di San Francesco, among the region's greatest 13th-century artists, and was painted in tempera and gold on wood. The painting highlights the suffering of Christ by portraying his head reclined over his shoulder and his body arched on the cross.

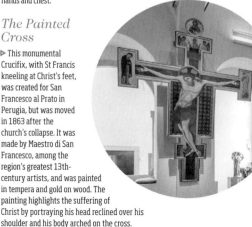

Palazzo dei Priori overlooking the Fontana Maggiore, Piazza IV Novembre

EXPERIENCE MORE

6

Umbertide

 C2 24 km (15 miles) S of
Città di Castello FCU
Perugia-Sansepolcro line
Via Mancini 17; www.
comune.umbertide.pg.it

One of the principal centres
of the Upper Tiber Valley,
Umbertide is of ancient origin,
dating back to the 6th century
BCE, and was probably
founded by the Etruscans. The
town, skirted to the west by the
Tiber, frequently found itself at
the centre of wars and suffered
the resulting destruction and
sackings. In 1863, the town's
traditional name of Fratta was
replaced by Umbertide

TOP 5 WALKING
TRAILS
AROUND
UMBERTIDE

**Cascate Torrente
Carpina**
Passing by a waterfall,
this 10-km (6-mile) hike
leads to Rocca d'Aries.

**Umbertide to
Monte Corona**
This four-hour hike
climbs to a Romanesque
abbey and offers views
across the Apennines.

Anello del Faldo
Following the flow of
the Tiber, this 3-km
(1.8-mile) path goes to
Laghi di Faldo and back.

**Pian D'Assino to
Serra Partucci**
This 5-km (3-mile) walk
follows an old railway
track to a former mill.

**Umbertide to
Mount Acuto**
This 11-km (7 mile) hike
takes you to the summit
of Mount Acuto.

---

in honour of the sons of
Umberto Ranieri, who rebuilt
the town after the devastation
caused by the Lombard
invasions of 790 CE.

Much more recently, the
centre of the old town was
badly damaged by bombard-
ments during World War II.
Even so, many important
buildings survive. Two of
these overlook the vast
Piazza Mazzini, northwest of
the town centre: La Rocca, a
14th-century fortress inserted
into the walls and now a centre
for contemporary art, and the
16th-century church of Santa
Maria della Reggia. The church
was designed by Galeazzo
Alessi and Giulio Danti. Inside,
among the canvases that
decorate the tambour (the wall
below the dome), note the one
above the organ, an *Ascension
to Heaven* by Pomarancio.

Other important works to be
found in the town's churches
include an early 16th-century
fresco by Pinturicchio, in the
lunette of the doorway to the
church of Santa Maria della
Pietà (north of the old town,
outside the walls), and, in
particular, a *Deposition* by

Luca Signorelli in the Baroque
church of **Santa Croce**, in
the southern (and oldest)
part of the town, in Piazza
San Francesco. Due to the
importance of the Signorelli
painting – it is the only one by
the Cortona artist still to be
found in its original setting –
the church is now a museum.
In the same square are two
other churches: San Francesco
(13th–14th centuries) and San
Bernardino (18th century).

The countryside around
Umbertide is scattered with
fortifications, lasting evidence
of the region's great strategic
military importance. Along the
road to Preggio, 15 km (9 miles)
southwest of Umbertide,
is the Rocca di Preggio, one
of the principal strongholds
in the area, dating from the
10th century. Also of note
along this route are the castles
of Romeggio and Polgeto.

A couple of kilometres south
of town, along the River Tiber, a
road climbs up to the Badia
Monte Corona, a Romanesque
abbey with an underground
crypt. Climbing still higher,
you reach the 16th-century
hermitage and pretty village of
San Giuliana, set in a panoramic
position, and restored to its
medieval appearance.

Santa Croce
Piazza San
Francesco 075 9420147
10am–6pm Tue–Sun

7

Montone

🅰 C2 🚗 20 km (12 miles)
S of Città di Castello
🚆 Umbertide, 13 km
(8 miles), FCU Perugia-
Sansepolcro line 🚌
🅸 Piazza Fortebraccio 1;
www.comunemontone.it

One of Italy's most beautiful villages, Montone was built on two hilltops on the left bank of the Tiber. It is the first village of historical interest on the road running south through the Upper Tiber Valley. Established as a fortified site in the Middle Ages, Montone is still enclosed within its medieval walls, which are pierced by three gates: Porta del Verziere, Porta di Borgo Vecchio and Porta del Monte. The names correspond to the districts into which the castle was divided.

The medieval village is home to several buildings of interest. On the road leading up to the centre of Montone is the 16th-century church of the Madonna delle Grazie, as well as the oldest church in the village, the Romanesque Pieve di San Gregorio, dating from the 11th century.

Beyond the walls, it is worth visiting the 14th-century Gothic church of San Francesco. Along with the attached monastery, this is now home to the **Museo Comunale**. The fine doorway of the museum is made of inlaid wood. Inside, the building contains several valuable works of art by Italian painter Bartolomeo Caporali. Above the votive altar are frescoes of the Fortebraccio family and also a painting depicting the *Madonna del Soccorso*.

The church, which has a 16th-century wooden choir, once housed a *Madonna in Gloria* by Luca Signorelli. This is now in the National Gallery in London. The former monastery also houses an ethnographic museum, **Museo Etnografico**.

Students of Italian history should consider visiting the **Archivio Storico Comunale**, one of the most important historical archives in Umbria, with papal bulls and other important documents. It is housed in the former convent of Santa Caterina.

The countryside around Montone offers plenty of opportunities for walking, particularly along the course of the Torrente Carpina, which skirts the village to the east and joins the Tiber at Umbertide. On its banks is the Rocca d'Aries, a fortress with

↑ Breathtaking views of the countryside from the village of Montone

Byzantine origins that was renovated in the Renaissance era. Today, it is open for concerts and exhibitions and offers marvellous views over the Valle del Carpina.

Museo Comunale and Museo Etnografico

🚫🕙🏠 🅰 Ex Convento di San Francesco 📞 0759 306 535 🕙 Hours vary, call ahead

Archivio Storico Comunale

🅰 Via Alfredo Caseti 📞 0759 306 101 🚫 For renovation until further notice, call ahead for details

← The fortified town of Umbertide overlooking the Tiber

STAY

La Locanda del Capitano

Housed in a 12th-century palazzo, this country hotel has an on-site gourmet restaurant and a rooftop garden.

🅰 C2 🅰 Via Roma 7, Montone 🆆 ilcapitano.com

€€€

8

Città della Pieve

B4 **43 km (27 miles) SW of Perugia** **Chiusi-Chianciano, 10 km (6 miles), Florence-Rome line** **Piazza Matteotti; www. cittadellapieve.org**

Famous as the birthplace of the great Renaissance painter, Pietro Vannucci (who was known as Perugino and taught the young Raphael), this town is worth a visit because it houses several of the artist's major works.

An Etruscan colony of Chiusi (in nearby Tuscany), and later Roman, Città della Pieve developed as a fortified town in about 1000, around the church of Santi Gervasio e Protasio. The red coloration is due to the use of bricks, as stones weren't available then.

Did You Know?

Perugino used saffron from Città della Pieve as a dye for his canvases and frescoes.

Città della Pieve features some of the narrowest streets in Italy, such as Vicolo Baciadonne, which is just 80 cm (31 in) wide. At the town's centre is the Piazza del Plebiscito with the Palazzo della Corgna (with 16th-century frescoes by Pomarancio), the Biblioteca Comunale (library) and the cathedral of Santi Gervasio e Protasio. The cathedral has precious works of art by Domenico Alfani, Giannicola di Paolo and Pomarancio, and there are also paintings by Perugino.

Visitors will find beautiful frescoes by Perugino in the church of Santa Maria dei Bianchi, in Corso Vannucci, just off Piazza del Plebiscito. One of them depicts the *Adoration of the Magi* (1504), and is perhaps the best of all the works by Perugino.

9

Nocera Umbra

E3 **42 km (26 miles) SE of Gubbio** **Nocera Scalo, 3 km (2 miles), Rome-Ancona line** **Pro Loco, Via San Rinaldo 9; www. nocerainumbria.it**

High on a rocky outcrop, Nocera Umbra was an ancient

THE WATERS OF NOCERA

Since the 18th century, the mineral-water springs in the Nocera area were used as a benchmark for measuring the purity of other waters. Their curative powers derive from the combination of a water that is particularly pure and mineral rich in itself, and the clay typical of this terrain. The two main springs can be found at Bagni di Nocera and at Schiagni (Fonte del Cacciatore).

Umbrian town called Nuokria, which was an important settlement under both the Romans and the Lombards. The waters that gush from the many springs (Bagni di Nocera) in the area are known for their curative properties.

In the charming historic centre stands the 11th-century Torre Civico or "Campanaccio", which sustained major damage from the earthquake of 1997 but has since been restored to its full splendour. The 14th-century church of San Francesco in Piazza Caprera is home to the Pinacoteca Comunale and Museo Civico, which display religious artifacts and works of art by Pierino Cesarei, Giulio Cesare Angeli and Ercole Ramazzani.

The Museo Archeologico nearby holds collections dedicated to important finds in the area over the centuries. The Palazzo Camilli, meanwhile, houses the CEDAT, a research centre dedicated to the history of Bagni di Nocera and the elements characterizing the famous waters.

Further afield is the peak of Monte Pennino (1,571 m/ 5,155 ft), on the Le Marche border, 20 km (12 miles) from Nocera Umbra. This scenic mountain has opportunities for hiking and skiing.

↑ A charming narrow street in Città della Pieve

Medieval-era buildings surrounded by greenery in Gualdo Tadino ↑

Gualdo Tadino

🅐 E3 🚗 30 km (18 miles) SE of Gubbio 🚆 Foligno-Ancona line 🚌 Piazza Orti Mavarelli 🛈 Associazione Pro Tadino, Piazza Martiri della Libertà 4; www.turismo.tadino.it

This town of ancient Umbrian and Roman origins took shape in the Middle Ages, but was heavily modified over hundreds of years, and today bears only a few traces of its past. Nevertheless, Gualdo is still one of the key centres of majolica manufacture in Umbria.

The town is home to several sights of interest, including San Benedetto, the only ancient gate to have survived over the centuries, and the Piazza XX Settembre, home to the medieval-era churches of San Donato and Santa Maria dei Raccomandati.

Another highlight is the church of San Francesco, which has an elegant Gothic doorway. Inside, there are many frescoes, most of which are the work of Matteo da Gualdo, the best-known artist native to the town. His works can also be seen in Assisi and Spoleto. The fresco on the first pilaster on the left, of *St Anne, the Virgin and Child*, is said to be his oldest work.

The central Piazza Martiri della Libertà, better known locally as Piazza Grande, features the town's principal buildings. Towering over the space is the 12th-century Palazzo Comunale, which was rebuilt after a terrible earthquake in 1751. Opposite is the 13th-century Palazzo del Podestà. The palazzo hosts an international ceramics exhibition and competition every year in July, which draws dozens of ceramic workers.

The elegant cathedral of San Benedetto stands on the eastern side of Piazza Martiri. Its façade has three doors, a beautiful rose window and a number of 20th-century frescoes. Outside the cathedral, to the left, stands a lovely Renaissance fountain.

Perched atop one of the hills surrounding Gualdo Tadino is the 10th-century **Rocca Flea**. This fortress houses an art gallery, a ceramics gallery and a collection of archaeological finds. The former showcases detached frescoes by Matteo da Gualdo as well as works by Jacopo Palma, Antonio da Fabriano and Niccolò Alunno.

Rocca Flea

🎨 🕙 🏠 Piazza della Rocca 📞 3477541791 🕙 10am-1pm, 3-6pm 🚫 1 Jan, 25 Dec

EAT

Osteria Panicaglia
This stylish restaurant is housed in an old castle.

🅐 E3 🏠 Località Panicaglia, Nocera Umbra borgocastello panicaglia.com

€€€

Trattoria Bruno Coppetta
Enjoy great seasonal fare at this long-standing restaurant.

🅐 B4 🏠 Via Pietro Vannucci 90/92, Città della Pieve 🌐 trattoria brunocoppetta.com

€€€

DRINK

Enoteca Fibonacci
This cosy wine bar has an extensive list of vintages, accompanied by live music on weekends.

🅐 B4 🏠 Piazza A Gramsci 1, Città della Pieve enoteca-fibonacci.business.site

Abbey of Vallingegno
on a verdant hilltop,
a few miles from Gubbio ↑

A LONG WALK
THE FRANCISCAN PATH OF PEACE

Distance 51 km (32 miles) **Stopping-off points**
Valfabbrica **Terrain** Mix of tarmac and gravel road;
some hilly terrain **Nearest station** Assisi railway station
Information www.ilsentierodifrancesco.it

Of the many trails traversing Umbria, this one is by far
the most popular. Covering a section of the much longer
Via di Francesco, it retraces part of the journey taken by
St Francis (p108) in 1206. Along the way, the saint decided
to abandon his life of comfort and privilege and dedicate
himself to the service of others. The route, which is hilly
but still reasonably easy to walk, links Assisi in Central
Umbria to Gubbio in Northern
Umbria, and loosely follows the
route that St Francis trod
around 800 years ago.

*Just before the route
ends at **Gubbio** is
the "Vittorina". This
church, dedicated to
Santa Maria della
Vittoria, is where it is
said that Francis
tamed the wolf.*

*Another notable
spiritual place is
the **Abbey of
Vallingegno**, a
Benedictine
centre from the
11th century.*

Pieve di Coccorano is one of
*many chapels that St Francis
must have encountered on
his journey, giving him the
chance to stop and pray.*

FINISH — Gubbio

MONTELOVESCO

PONTE D'ASSI

MENGARA

Abbey of Vallingegno

BISCINA

Church of Caprignone

STRADA PROVINCIALE DI CASA CASTALDA

Fiume Chiascio

Lago di Valfabbrica

Pieve di Coccorano

Abbey of Valfabbrica

PORZIANO

PIANELLO

Pieve San Nicolò

PALAZZO

VIA CAMPIGLIONE

SANTA MARIA DEGLI ANGEL

Assisi
START

NORTHERN UMBRIA

*The Franciscan
Path of Peace*

Locator Map

↑ The ancient Porta San
Giacomo near the Basilica
di San Francesco, Assisi

The **church of Caprignone**
*sums up the austerity of the
Franciscan Order. It hosted
the first chapter of the Order
convened outside Assisi in 1223.*

The **Abbey of Valfabbrica** may
*well have been the place where
St Francis stayed before
continuing to Gubbio.*

*After a hilly journey from Assisi,
you reach the pretty village of
Pieve San Nicolò. Both Assisi
and neighbouring Valfabbrica
can be seen from here.*

The trail starts from **Assisi's**
*Porta San Giacomo, probably
the gate through which St Francis
passed when he left the city.*

0 km   5

0 miles   5

N ↑

A CYCLING TOUR
SOUTHERN LAGO TRASIMENO

Distance 36 km (22 miles) **Stopping-off points**
Panicale, Tavernelle, Fontignano **Nearest bus stop**
Castiglione del Lago

In the mountains that rise to the south of Lago Trasimeno lies a series of villages where art and history have always played an important role. The painter Pietro Vannucci, better known as Perugino, was born in nearby Città della Pieve and worked in the area. Passing alongside farmland, this cycling tour partly retraces the steps of the great artist and partly seeks out small medieval hilltowns, which are among the great treasures of Umbria.

NORTHERN UMBRIA

Southern Lago Trasimeno

Locator Map

Lago Trasimeno

Sant Arcangelo

599

Panicarola

Cascina

Mácchie

Panicale

*Begin your pootle at **Paciano**. Surrounded by leafy woods and olive groves, it's one of the area's best-preserved medieval villages.*

Paciano
START

Tavernelle

Monte Pausillo 600 m (1,968 ft)

220 *Torrente Ierna*

A street in Paciano decorated with colourful umbrellas ↑

*The fortified town of **Panicale** is perched on a rocky spur. Perugino's Martyrdom of St Sebastian (1505) can be seen in the church of San Sebastiano.*

*Just north of the village of **Tavernelle** is the Santuario della Madonna di Mongiovino, a 16th-century church with frescoes from the same period.*

0 kilometres   4

0 miles   4

N ↑

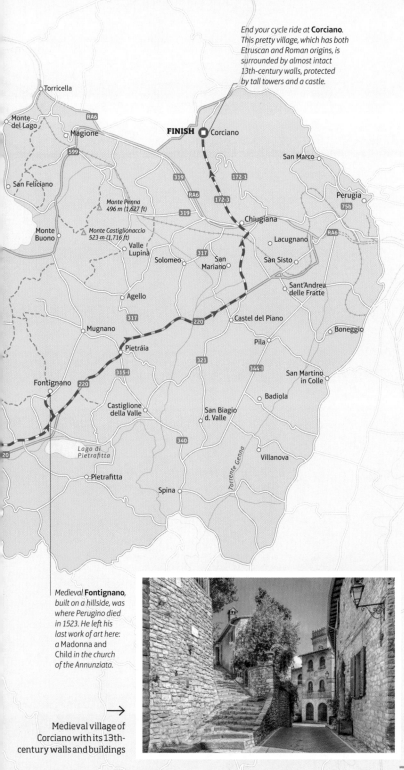

End your cycle ride at **Corciano**. This pretty village, which has both Etruscan and Roman origins, is surrounded by almost intact 13th-century walls, protected by tall towers and a castle.

Torricella

Monte del Lago

RA6

Magione

FINISH Corciano

San Marco

599

Perugia

San Feliciano

75b

Monte Penna
496 m (1,627 ft)

319

RA6

172-1

172-3

Chiugiana

Lacugnano

RA6

Monte Castiglionaccio
523 m (1,716 ft)

319

Monte Buono

Valle Lupina

Solomeo

317

San Mariano

San Sisto

Agello

Sant'Andrea delle Fratte

Mugnano

317

220

Castel del Piano

Boneggio

Pietráia

Pila

San Martino in Colle

321

344-1

Fontignano

220

315-1

Badiola

Castiglione della Valle

San Biagio d. Valle

Lago di Pietrafitta

340

Villanova

20

Torrente Genna

Pietrafitta

Spina

Medieval **Fontignano**, built on a hillside, was where Perugino died in 1523. He left his last work of art here: a Madonna and Child in the church of the Annunziata.

→

Medieval village of Corciano with its 13th-century walls and buildings

CENTRAL UMBRIA

As with its northern neighbour, Central Umbria is cut through by the River Tiber, which also separated its earliest peoples: the Umbri, who lived to its east, and the Etruscans, who settled to the river's west. The former established hilltop towns like Assisi, Spello and Todi around the 7th century BCE, while the latter set up Orvieto, carving an extensive network of caves beneath the city; these provided storage for wine, olive oil and other foods, as well as shelter during times of siege. It's unsurprising, then, that this was the last city in the Etruscan League to fall to the Romans in the 3rd century BCE. The Romans took over other towns and cities in Central Umbria, including Todi in the 3rd century BCE and Spello in the 1st century BCE.

During the 6th century CE, parts of the region, including Todi, fell under the control of the Lombard Duchy of Spoleto, with much of the area remaining under its rule during the early Middle Ages. In the 12th century, it became part of the Papal States, as did much of the rest of Umbria. Despite this, many cities here enjoyed extensive independence, with major building projects undertaken during this time; Orvieto's majestic Duomo, for instance, was founded at the end of the 13th century, as was Spello's Santa Maria Maggiore; Assisi's spectacular Basilica di San Francesco, meanwhile, was commissioned by Pope Gregory IX in 1228 to honour the town's most famous son, St Francis. While papal control intensified in the 14th century, the region continued to bloom under the Renaissance, with renowned painters decorating the likes of Orvieto's Duomo with masterful frescoes. It's sights like these that have made Central Umbria a magnet for tourists in the 20th and 21st centuries, with 5 million people visiting Assisi every year.

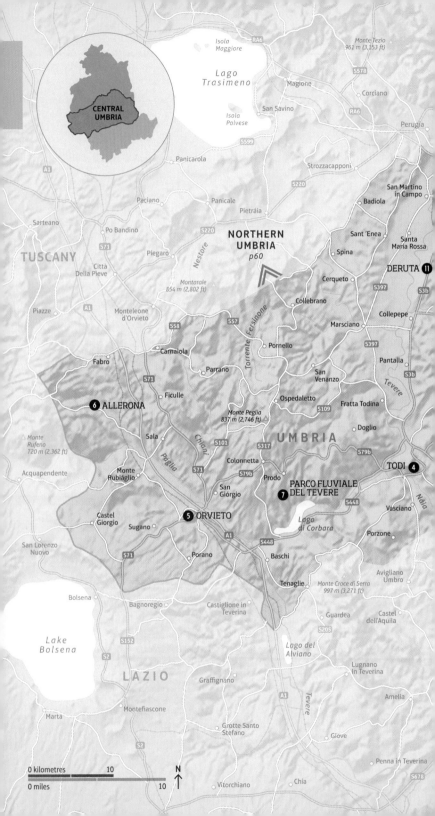

CENTRAL UMBRIA

Must Sees

1. Assisi
2. Parco Regionale del Monte Subasio
3. Spello
4. Todi
5. Orvieto

Experience More

6. Allerona
7. Parco Fluviale del Tevere
8. Torgiano
9. Bettona
10. Bevagna
11. Deruta
12. Foligno
13. Fonti del Clitunno
14. Trevi
15. Altopiano di Colfiorito
16. Montefalco

ASSISI

🗺 D4 🚗 27 km (17 miles) SE of Perugia via SS 75 🚉 Assisi (Piazza Matteotti); Stazione Assisi (Piazza Garibaldi), Foligno-Terontola line 🚌 APM ℹ Piazza del Comune; www.visit-assisi.it

Founded by the Umbrians, Assisi was prominent during the Roman era, and the town achieved more importance during the Middle Ages. By the time the Basilica of San Francesco was founded in the 13th century, Assisi had already taken shape, with two fortresses added a century later. Over the following centuries, the city changed little and today retains its medieval ambience.

💬 INSIDER TIP
Taking the Bus

When taking the bus from the railway station to town, get off at the end of the line (Parcheggio Saba Matteotti) instead of the Assisi Parcheggio Saba stop. You'll avoid a tiring uphill climb to the city's main square.

① Santa Chiara

🏛 Piazza Santa Chiara 📞 075 812216 🕙 9am-noon & 2-7pm daily (winter: to 6pm)

Assisi's second great church was begun in 1257, and consecrated eight years later by Pope Clement IV. The body of St Clare, founder of the order of the Poor Clares, was buried here in 1260.

The façade has a simple doorway with a rose window above, while the side that faces the street is supported by three vast buttresses. The church is distinctive because of the use of alternating layers of white and red stone, as seen in some Tuscan churches.

The interior is in the form of a Latin cross, simple and spare. In the right transept there is a cycle of frescoes depicting *Scenes from the Life of St Clare*, by an unknown artist called the Master of Santa Chiara. Other interesting frescoes, from the 14th century, can be found on the left wall, while on the right, in the Oratorio delle Reliquie, there is the late 12th-century wooden Crucifix of San Damiano. According to the hagiography, this is the crucifix that famously spoke to Francis in San Damiano, asking him to "repair his church".

② Duomo (San Rufino)

🏛 Piazza San Rufino 📞 075 812712 🕙 10am-1pm & 3-6pm Mon-Sat, 11am-6pm Sun

Built on a Roman religious site in around 1029 by Archbishop Ugone, the duomo was rebuilt in the 12th-13th centuries. The church was consecrated in 1253 by Pope Innocent IV.

The cathedral is worth a visit for its splendid façade, a masterpiece of Umbrian Romanesque. It is divided into three horizontal sections. At ground level are three doors decorated with lions; above are three rose windows with symbols of the Evangelists. At the top is a tympanum with a Gothic arch.

The interior dates from the 16th century. It still has the old

Picturesque view of the town of Assisi at sunset ↓

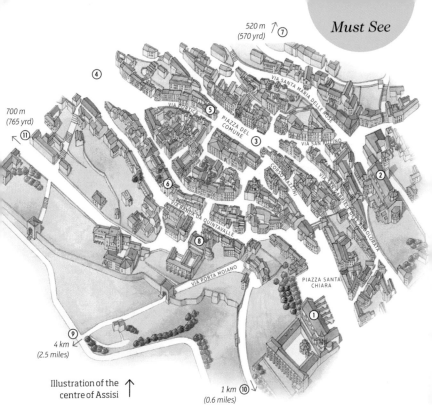

520 m ↑ ⑦
(570 yrd)

④

700 m
(765 yrd)
← ⑪

VIA SANTA MARIA DELLE ROSE

VIA PORTICO

⑤

PIAZZA DEL
COMUNE

③

VIA SAN RUFINO

②

⑥

CORSO MAZZINI

VIA GABRIELE D'ANNUNZIO

VIA BORGO DA QUINTAVALLE

⑧

VIA PORTA MOIANO

PIAZZA SANTA
CHIARA

①

Illustration of the
centre of Assisi ↑

⑨
4 km ↙
(2.5 miles)

1 km ⑩ ↘
(0.6 miles)

---

baptismal font where St Francis and St Clare were baptized.

Adjacent to the church is the Museo della Cattedrale (cathedral museum), which contains pieces from the original church, a series of frescoes from the Oratorio di San Rufinuccio and paintings from various churches in Assisi. In the church courtyard a plaque shows the site of the house where St Clare was born.

---

③

Piazza del Comune

Created in its current form in the 13th century, this square has always been the true heart of the city. The main focus of the piazza is the **Temple of Minerva**, built in the 1st century BCE on a set of terraces that once marked the axis of the town. This beautifully preserved Roman temple – complete with towering Corinthian columns – has changed function at various

times over the centuries: it was first a church, then a group of shops, then seat of the town hall. In 1456, it finally became a place of worship again, with the name of Santa Maria sopra Minerva. In the 16th century, its interior was completely remodelled into the Baroque style that is still seen today – something that provides a striking contrast to the building's Roman exterior.

On the left of the temple portico is the 13th-century Palazzo del Capitano del Popolo. The Fonte di Piazza, at the far end of the square, is an 18th-century fountain built on the foundations of a 13th-century water basin.

A descent through the Arco dei Priori leads to **Chiesa Nuova**, which was commissioned by

Philip III of Spain to mark the spot where St Francis was said to have been born.

Temple of Minerva
🏠 Piazza del Comune 📞 0758 12361 🕒 7:15am–7:30pm Mon–Sat, 8am–7:30pm Sun & hols

Chiesa Nuova
🏠 Piazzetta Chiesa Nuova 7 📞 0758 12339 🕒 8am– 12:30pm & 2:30–6pm daily

→
Baroque-style vault
and high altar of the
Temple of Minerva

EAT

Osteria Piazzetta dell'Erba

An innovative spot, this osteria offers three menus, covering traditional Umbrian, fusion and sushi.

 Via Gabriele Ⓦosteriapiazzetta dellerba.it

€€€

Le Terrazze di Properzio

This welcoming restaurant offers homemade pasta and commanding views from its hillside terrace.

 Via Metastasio 9 Ⓦle-terrazze-di-properzio.business.site

€€€

La Locanda del Cardinale

Enjoy fine dining at this upscale spot, home to a glass floor that looks down on the remains of a Roman *domus*.

 Piazza del Vescovado 8 Ⓦlalocandadel cardinale.com

€€€

DRINK

Enoteca Mazzini

Located in the historic centre of Assisi, this wine cellar serves up over 1,500 labels.

Corso Mazzini 16 ☎07581 6383

Wine Assisi Tesori dell'Umbria

This friendly spot offers a range of wines.

Via Frate Elia 1B ☎3755 104 865

Via San Francesco

Head towards the Basilica di San Francesco to cover the whole length of Via del Seminario, which becomes Via San Francesco. Along the way pass the 17th-century Palazzo Giacobetti and, opposite, the delightful 15th-century **Oratorio dei Pellegrini**, once part of a pilgrim's hospice, followed by the arches of the Portico del Monte Frumentario, part of a 13th-century hospital. Next comes the Palazzo Vallemani, which is the temporary home of the **Pinacoteca Comunale**; the art gallery's most important work is probably the *Madonna in Maestà* (Giotto school), found near the entrance. A little further along is the Loggia dei Maestri Comacini, a 13th-century *palazzetto* which, according to tradition, was the seat of the Lombard rulers; it is adorned with a 15th-century coats of arms. Nearby, the steep Vicolo di Sant'Andrea climbs up to the Piazza di Santa Margherita, from where there are classic views towards the Basilica di San Francesco. It is especially moving at sunset or at dawn.

Oratorio dei Pellegrini

Via San Francesco 13 ☎075812267 ⏱9am-noon & 4-6pm Mon-Sat

Pinacoteca Comunale

Palazzo Vallemani, Via San Francesco 12 ☎0758158 680 ⏱10am-6pm Wed-Sun

---

⑤

Museo and Foro Romano

Via Portica 2 ☎0758 138 680 ⏱10am-7pm daily

On the corner of Piazza del Comune, beyond the Arco del Seminario – the ancient limit of the walled city in the Roman era – is a museum of Roman finds. Inside, visitors can gain access to the ruins found beneath the modern square, which may have been a Roman forum.

Following the museum's long corridor, which leads directly underneath the piazza, is a room where three marble statues unearthed in Assisi are kept; one is believed to depict the goddess Minerva.

←

Statue from the archaeological collection at the Museo and Foro Romano

Via Frate Elia, leading on to the church of San Pietro

The fortress was built in the 12th century and was used by Duke Corrado di Urslingen (who was tutor to the future Emperor Frederick II). It was destroyed and rebuilt more than once, including by Cardinal Albornoz in 1367, from which period most of what is now visible dates. Later additions include the polygonal tower in 1458 and the round tower by the entrance.

PICTURE PERFECT
Punto Panoramico

At sunset, head to the Punto Panoramico, which is a short walk from the grounds of the Rocca Maggiore. This scenic viewpoint is the perfect spot from which to capture the Upper Basilica of St Francis illuminated by the rays of the setting sun.

> The church of San Pietro, along with the adjacent monastery, was founded by the Benedictines in the 10th century... and was consecrated in 1254.

⑥
San Pietro

⌂ Piazza San Pietro
☎ 0755 094 993
🕑 Daily

The church of San Pietro, along with the adjacent monastery, was founded by the Benedictines in the 10th century. It is just a short walk from the Basilica di San Francesco along Via Frate Elia to San Pietro. The existing church dates from the same period as the Basilica of St Francis, and was consecrated in 1254.

The striking Romanesque-Gothic façade of the church was originally decorated with a pediment, taken down in the 19th century. The interior is mainly Romanesque. Its distinguishing features are its sober simplicity and the height of its nave.

⑦
Rocca Maggiore

⌂ Via della Rocca
☎ 0758 138 680
🕑 10am–8pm daily

This well-preserved fortress stands at the northern edge of the city, reached by walking up Via di Porta Perlici from Piazza San Rufino. The panorama, overlooking the Valle del Tescio, the Valle Umbra and Assisi itself, with the façade of the duomo in the foreground, more than compensates for the effort of the climb.

↑ Exhibits at the 12th-century fortress, Rocca Maggiore

Santa Maria Maggiore

⊠ Piazza del Vescovo 3
☎ 0758 13085 ⏱ Summer: 7am-7pm daily; winter: 8am-7pm daily

Built on the site of an older church, which was in turn erected atop a Roman temple, this simple yet beautiful 10th-century church was Assisi's first cathedral. It was rebuilt in Romanesque form around 1163, with a Gothic-Romanesque bell tower added sometime in the 14th century.

The building's Romanesque origins are reflected in the unadorned façade, whose only decoration is a rose window. Inside, from the crypt there is access to what is supposed to be the House of Propertius (Casa di Properzio), the great Roman poet (c.50–16 BCE). However, this has not been confirmed; in fact, at least three Umbrian cities – Assisi, Spello and Bevagna – have claimed to be the famous poet's birthplace.

Santa Maria degli Angeli-Porziuncola

⊠ Santa Maria degli Angeli
☎ 0758 0511 ⏱ 7:30am-12:30pm & 3-6:45pm daily

Another place that was dear to Francis is at the bottom of the hill (through the Porta San Pietro). Built at the end of the 16th century, the church of Santa Maria degli Angeli (the seventh-largest church in the world) was, in fact, designed to accommodate the buildings of the 11th-century Porziuncola ("the little portion"), the chapel where St Francis lived and which was the centre of the early Franciscan Order. In 1569, Pope Pius IV laid the first stone of the vast Santa Maria, constructed to receive hordes of pilgrims. The project was given to Galeazzo Alessi, and work was concluded more than a century later with the building of the great cupola and one of the two bell towers.

Inside the vast church, beneath the dome, is the old oratory, known as the Cappella della Porziuncola; on the right is the Cappella del Transito, the old infirmary cell where St Francis died on 4 October 1226; the door is original. This chapel contains a majolica statue of St Francis

POOR CLARES, FRANCISCAN NUNS AND CAPUCHIN NUNS

The origin of the Order of Poor Clares (Clarisse) dates back to when St Clare (Santa Chiara) took the veil, celebrated by St Francis in 1212 at what is now Santa Maria degli Angeli-Porziuncola. She left with a group of sisters and went to the church of San Damiano, where she decided to follow in the footsteps of St Francis by establishing a female Franciscan Order. The Rule of the Poor Clares was drawn up in 1224 by Francis and was observed by St Clare. In the 15th century, the Reformed Franciscan Order of nuns was established, and in 1525 a female branch of the Capuchin Order was founded. The three orders survive to this day.

by Andrea della Robbia. Also of note is the Cappella del Roseto (chapel of the rose garden), with early 16th-century frescoes by Tiberio d'Assisi. The chapel takes its name from a legend, according to which St Francis rolled naked on the roses in the

garden (to mortify his body), only to find that all the thorns immediately vanished.

In the convent there is a small museum, with a painted *Crucifix* by Giunta Pisano (mid-13th century) and a painting of *St Francis* by an unknown artist who later passed into history as the Maestro di San Francesco.

About 5 km (3 miles) south of Assisi, on the road to Foligno, is the imposing **Santuario di Rivotorto**, built in 1854 in Neo-Gothic style on the site of a stone hut where the first community of Franciscan friars lived briefly, in 1209; St Francis wrote the first set of rules for his Order here. On the façade are the symbols of the Basilica di San Francesco. Also in Rivotorto is the peaceful British and Commonwealth "Assisi War Graves" cemetery.

Santuario di Rivotorto

📍 Rivotorto di Assisi, 5 km (3 miles) 📞 0758 065 432
🕐 7am-7:30pm daily

Did You Know?

A replica of Santa Maria degli Angeli-Porziuncola, known as La Nuova Porziuncola, is located in San Francisco.

Sanctuary of San Damiano

📍 Via San Damiano 7
🕐 6:15am-noon & 2-7:45pm daily (winter: to 5:45pm)
🌐 santuariosandamiano.org

The Franciscan church of San Damiano is one of the most significant places in the life of St Francis. It was here that, in 1205, the saint said he heard the words: "Francis, go and repair my church which is falling down". According to the great chronicler of Francis' life, Tommaso da Celano, the words were spoken by the crucifix which is now in the Basilica di Santa Chiara (p102). The building indicated by the crucifix was that of the church of San Damiano. Francis, together with a few faithful followers, undertook the restoration.

St Francis brought St Clare to San Damiano; she and her first followers congregated here, and founded the convent in which St Francis composed his *Canticle of the Creatures*. Today, the convent is run by the Order of the Frati Minori Osservanti (Friars Minor).

The sanctuary is worth a visit from both an architectural and artistic point of view, especially for the convent rooms: the Oratorio di Santa Chiara, the cloister and the refectory.

← Entrance to the church of Santa Maria degli Angeli-Porziuncola, and *(inset)* its frescoed interior

↑ Beautiful garden at the Sanctuary of San Damiano

SHOP

Il Lavandeto di Assisi
This charming shop sells lavender-scented goods, such as soaps and oils, from plants sourced from a local nursery.

📍 Via Portica 16 🌐 il lavandetodiassisi.com

Tipografia Libreria Zubboli
Find handcrafted artisanal paper, art blocks, pens and leather-bound notebooks at this stationery shop.

📍 Piazza del Comune 18 🌐 zubboli.com

Galleria d'Arte San Francesco
Housed in an old stone building, this gallery showcases works by local artists, as well as a collection of ancient prints and antique marble tabletops.

📍 Via A Fortini 10 a/b 🌐 sanfrancescoarte.info

BASILICA DI SAN FRANCESCO

🏛Piazza San Francesco 2 ⏲Upper Church: 8:30am–6:45pm daily; Lower Church: 6am–6pm daily 🌐sanfrancescoassisi.org

Dominating the northwestern side of Assisi, this arresting basilica – a mix of Gothic and Romanesque styles – was built to honour St Francis. Today, it remains a major site of pilgrimage and is home to some of the region's most spectacular frescoes.

Just 18 months after the death of St Francis, Frate Elia (Brother Elias), Vicar-General of the Franciscan Order, was tasked by Pope Gregory IX with building a church dedicated to the saint. After the laying of the first stone, the Lower Church was the first part to take shape; the Upper Church was eventually built on top of it. The basilica was consecrated by Pope Innocent IV in 1253, though the chapel of Santa Caterina, the final stage in the basilica's construction, was not completed until 1367. Some of the greatest artists of the age left their mark on the building: works by Cimabue and Pietro Lorenzetti adorn the older church, while the newer, larger one is famed for its beautiful frescoes by Giotto. The basilica is also home to the much-venerated tomb of St Francis, which today is visited by modern-day pilgrims.

THE LIFE OF ST FRANCIS

Giovanni di Pietro di Bernardone was born in Assisi in 1182 to a well-off family. In his early 20s, he had a series of visions that he believed were from God, leading him to take a vow to live a life of poverty and renunciation. Alongside his followers he rejected the wealth and seclusion of monastic orders, instead ministering to the urban poor. He was canonized following his death in 1226, becoming the patron saint of Italy, and of the environment, due to his love for all God's creatures.

The wooden choir is an example of Gothic Renaissance engraving and inlaid wood.

The walls of the transept are decorated with an outstanding cycle of frescoes painted by Cimabue and his assistants. The Crucifixion in the left transept is superb.

The celebrated allegorical frescoes of the Quattro Vele (vault above the altar), in the Lower Church, represent The Three Virtues of St Francis.

The Tomb of St Francis, in the crypt, was discovered only in 1818. The remains of the saint were transferred here in 1230, before the basilica was finished.

Cross-section of the Basilica di San Francesco ↑

1 The frescoes in the Cappella di San Martino depict scenes from the life of St Martin.

2 The exquisite interior of the Upper Church takes the forms of French Gothic.

3 The basilica has a simple and elegant façade.

The Cappella di San Martino, the first on the left in the Lower Church, was decorated by Simone Martini.

The vault in the nave is decorated with frescoes by various masters.

The soaring, single-nave Upper Church is typical of Franciscan monastic architecture.

The façade is an example of Italian Gothic. It has a double rose window in Cosmatesque style and a double door.

The left side of the crossing was decorated by Pietro Lorenzetti. This is one of two portraits of the Madonna and Child.

The frescoes on the Life of St Francis, on the lower walls of the nave, are attributed to a superb unknown artist, often referred to as the Maestro di San Francesco.

Exploring the basilica

Two buildings, the Lower Church and the Upper Church, combine to form the basilica. The smaller and simpler Lower Church was designed to function as the saint's burial place and to accommodate pilgrims, while the Upper Church was for regular worship. Both buildings are decorated with impressive cycles of frescoes, created by some of the greatest painters of the age. Today, the building is regarded as one of the finest and most loved monuments in the history of Western art.

Lower Church

Darker and more contemplative, the Lower Church retains its original Romanesque style. Its design mirrors that of a cavernous crypt, with side chapels dedicated to several saints. Every inch of the ribbed vaults is adorned with frescoes by medieval masters. Underneath the Lower Church, the tomb of St Francis is reached via a double staircase. Rediscovered in 1818, his remains were hidden here by the original basilica architect Brother Elias, to ensure that his relics were not dispersed across Europe.

$\longrightarrow$

A rose window and frescoes on the cross-vaulted ceiling adorn the entrance

> The Upper Church is one of Umbria's most beautiful buildings, thanks to its soaring walls, which are adorned with some of the most important frescoes in the history of early medieval Italian art.

Upper Church

This part of the basilica is one of Umbria's most beautiful buildings, thanks to its cross-vaulted ceiling, painted blue and decorated with stars, and its soaring walls, which are adorned with some of the most important frescoes in the history of early medieval Italian art.

The pictorial decoration of the Upper Church is divided into two main sections: the frescoes of the apse, transept and the crossing, by Cimabue and his school; and those of the nave and vaults, where episodes from the Old and New Testaments are portrayed alongside representations of the life of St Francis. The latter, attributed to 13th-century Florentine artist and architect Giotto, depict with tenderness and detail the major events in the life of the saint. They are seminal examples of the use of perspective, a definitive break with flat Byzantine style and a precursor to the sense of humanity that would define Renaissance art.

TOP 3 FRESCO PAINTERS

Cimabue
This Florence-born artist was among the first to break with flat, emotionless Byzantine style and depict more proportionate, lifelike figures.

Pietro Lorenzetti
The Siena-born artist is known for his use of three-dimensions and emotion, especially in his works in the Lower Basilica.

Giotto
Regarded as the father of the Renaissance and an alleged pupil of Cimabue, Giotto marshalled the transition from the Gothic to Proto-Renaissance styles.

↑ The transepts and apse of the Upper Church featuring frescoes by Cimabue

❷

PARCO REGIONALE DEL MONTE SUBASIO

🅐D4 **🅐** Park entrance 1 km (less than a mile) E of Assisi **🚉** Assisi, Foligno-Terontola line **🚌** APM Assisi-Eremo delle Carceri **ℹ** Loc Cà Piombino, Assisi; www.parks.it

Rising to the east of Assisi, the mountainous Parco Regionale del Monte Subasio is carpeted by lush woodlands and flower-flecked meadows, and home to sights of religious and historical significance.

This regional park takes its name from the dome-shaped Monte Subasio, which stands at 1,290 m (4,230 ft). It's possible to drive to the summit from Assisi, following a route that retraces an ancient cart track. The peak – which affords great views over the surrounding countryside – can also be reached on foot via several hiking trails. Some trails wind though the park's leafy forest, while others pass through pastures lined with olive trees. As well as mountain biking, horse riding and paragliding opportunities, there's also the chance to spy a range of wildlife, including birds of prey such as buzzards and goshawks; more elusive inhabitants include badgers, wild boars and wolves.

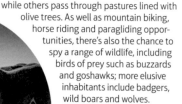

 GREAT VIEW
Bird's-Eye Views

Fly like an eagle with Parapendio in Due (*www.parapendio indue.it*). Accompanied by an expert instructor, you'll paraglide through the air, taking in spectacular views across both the mountainous park and Assisi.

↑ Tranquil setting of the 13th-century hermitage, Eremo delle Carceri

Exploring the park

The park is known for its religious ties, especially to St Francis, Italy's patron saint, who retreated here to take inspiration from nature and to pray. Tucked away among dense woodland is the Eremo delle Carceri (Hermitage of the Prisons), where Franciscan friars would "lock themselves away" in meditative prayer. It is also home to a 15th-century church, as well as a cave where St Francis would go to rest. Beyond the hermitage is a bridge that leads to a forest containing a series of caves and hermitages used in the Middle Ages by the devout and by friars. Other important sights include the fortified villages of Castello di Armenzano and Collepino, and the ancient fortification of Rocca di Postignano.

↑ Hiking through the park's wonderfully verdant forest

STAY

B&B Il Sentiero di Armenzano
Set along the Franciscan paths, this farmhouse is home to three comfortable en-suite rooms.

Localita Armenzano Ⓦilsentierodi armenzano.it

€€€

Le Silve di Armenzano Natural Resort
A luxe property in a former 11th-century hostel, Le Silve features a pool, a wellness spa and a zero-km kitchen on site.

Localita Armenzano 89 Ⓦlesilve.it

€€€

↑ Snowcapped Monte Subasio, and *(inset)* horses in the meadow

A cluster of medieval buildings in the beautiful town of Spello ↑

3

SPELLO

🅐 D4 🚋 12 km (7.5 miles) S of Assisi 🚉 Rome-Ancona line
ℹ️ Pro Loco, Piazza Matteotti 3; 0742 301 009

Founded by the Umbri in the shadow of Monte Subasio, Spello grew in size under the Romans, while the town walls were built in the Augustan era. Later, it was sacked by the Lombards, and then crushed again by Frederick II. Today, Spello is an important agricultural hub with numerous historic sights and lively summer events that draw in visitors.

① Pinacoteca Civica

🏛️ Piazza Matteotti 10
📞 0742 301 497 🕐 Apr-Sep: 10:30am-1:30pm & 3:30-5:30pm Fri-Sun

Since 1994 the civic art gallery has been housed in the Palazzo dei Canonici (15th century), to the right of Santa Maria Maggiore. Among the varied works in the collection, one highlight is a splendid *Wooden Madonna* dating from around 1240, brightly coloured and yet serene and stately. Also of note are several polyptychs of the 14th and 15th centuries and other significant works of the local school.

② Sant'Andrea

🏛️ Via Cavour

Near the Pinacoteca, the church of Sant'Andrea (13th century) has a rather gloomy interior; and yet in the right transept is a superb fresco by Pinturicchio of the *Madonna and Child with Saints*. In the left transept, look out for the mummified body of Andrea Caccioli, one of the first followers of St Francis.

③ Piazza della Repubblica

In this square at the end of Via Cavour is the 13th-century Palazzo Comunale (now restored), which contains the Library and the Town Archive.

Head north along Via Garibaldi to pass the Palazzo Cruciani, seat of the town council, and then the 12th-century church of San Lorenzo, an architectural hotchpotch. Of interest inside is the carved wooden pulpit, the work of Francesco Costantini (1600).

④ Santa Maria Maggiore

🏛️ Piazza Matteotti

Completed in 1285, this church is the most important monument in Spello. Its façade was reconstructed, using the original materials, in the 17th century.

The single-nave church owes its fame to the Cappella Baglioni, where there is a series of frescoes by Pinturicchio, perhaps the finest ever done

of the *Magi* and a *Dispute in the Temple*. The floor of the chapel was made of majolica tiles from Deruta. More Pinturicchio frescoes can be found in the Cappella del Sacramento, reached from the left transept. In the right transept is the Cappella del Sepolcro, which at one time housed the town art gallery. Also of interest are a pulpit in sandstone and a tabernacle on the high altar. The church canopy suffered some damage after the earthquake of 2016.

Porta dell'Arce

🏠 Via Arco Romano

One of the oldest entrances to the town, this gate is an example of how Roman buildings were integrated into the medieval fortifications. Nearby is the terrace of the Belvedere, from which the Topino valley, as well as the outline of Assisi's Santa Maria degli Angeli, can be admired.

by the artist. Painted from 1500–1501, the frescoes depict the *Four Sibyls* (on the vault) and *Scenes from the Life of Christ* (on the walls). The most important frescoes are an *Annunciation* (under which hangs a self-portrait of Pinturicchio), an *Adoration*

Must See

STAY

Hotel Palazzo Bocci
The rooms and suites at this opulent hotel are equipped with jacuzzis.

🏠 Via Cavour 17
🅦 palazzobocci.com

€€€

Terme Francescane Village
This hotel's spa facilities are excellent.

🏠 Via delle Acque
🅦 termefrancescane.com

€€€

Domus Flora House
This cute-as-a-button house is located in Spello's centre.

🏠 Via San Martino 11
🅦 domusflora.eu

€€€

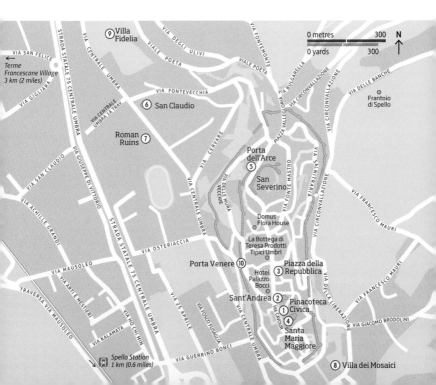

Limestone façade of the 12th-century church of San Claudio

⑥ San Claudio

🏛 Via Fontevecchia

From the Belvedere, you can descend to the plain via the narrow Via dei Cappuccini and then the long Via Fontevecchia. Here, you'll find the delightful church of San Claudio, dating from the 12th century. Perhaps Spello's most interesting church architecturally, it has retained intact its Romanesque decoration and layout. The simple façade of white limestone is somewhat asymmetrical and is topped by the original belfry. Inside the church is an altar made up of a pillar on which sits the upside-down marble lid of a Roman sarcophagus. The semicircular apse and the central nave are decorated with frescoes by artists from the 15th-century Umbrian school.

⑦ Roman Ruins

🏛 Via Centrale Umbra

These ruins are evidence of the ancient Roman settlement that once existed here, most likely built following the construction of the Via Flaminia in 219 BCE. It was built at a lower level than the medieval town, which was constructed more defensively on the hill. The amphitheatre, near the church of San Claudio on the main road to Foligno, dates from the 1st century CE, but little survives of the structure.

A kilometre (half a mile) from Spello towards Perugia is Villa Fidelia, which was once at the centre of the Roman city, and where an epigraph, known as the "Rescritto di Costantino" (rescript of Constantine), was found in 1733. According to this ordinance, in the years between 324 and 337 CE, the great emperor authorized the Umbrians to hold their celebrations at Spello and not in Orvieto. The marble tablet can now be admired in the Sala Zuccari inside the Palazzo Comunale Vecchio.

⑧ Villa dei Mosaici

🏛 Via Paolina Schicchi Fagotti 🕙 10am–7pm daily 🚫 Jan 1 🌐 villadei mosaicidispello.it

Beyond the city's main gate, Porta Consolare, are the remains of a 2nd-century CE Roman villa that was created at the height of the settlement's power. The villa features well-preserved mosaic floors bearing poly-chrome geometric motifs, which depict wild animals, mystical creatures and bountiful harvest scenes. Unearthed during the construction of a car park in 2005, it is believed to be one of the most extra-ordinary archaeological finds in the region. Visitors can enjoy virtual tours of

→

The Roman gateway, Porta Venere, with its two towers

INSIDER TIP
L'Infiorata di Spello

Visit the city during its annual flower festival, L'Infiorata di Spello, in June. At this time, the town's pink stone streets are carpeted with colourful petals in different designs that span 1 km (half a mile).

the site through its mobile phone app "Spello's Villa of Mosaics".

 ⑨
Villa Fidelia

🏛 **Via Villa Costanzi**

Set on a hill near the town's ancient ruins, the 17th-century Villa Fidelia was originally commissioned by the Urbani, a wealthy Spello family. It was acquired by aristocrat Teresa Pamphili Grillo in the 1700s, who dedicated herself to renovating the building and adding its beautiful Italian garden.

Bought and sold several times over, it was passed to engineer Decio Costanzi in 1923, who divided the property, selling one part to a nearby monastery and another to the Province of Perugia. Today, the garden functions as a park and features a cypress grove, parterres of rose gardens and, between terracotta steps, a fountain with an exedra capped by a statue of Diana, goddess of hunting.

⑩
Porta Venere

🏛 **Via Torri di Properzio**

A short detour west from Piazza della Repubblica takes you to Porta Venere, a Roman gateway flanked by two imposing 12-sided towers dating from the Middle Ages. The gate, heavily restored over the centuries, dates from the Augustan era: the structure that you see today originally had a double curtain giving way to an internal courtyard. The gate offers good views over the surrounding countryside.

Frantoio di Spello
Located at the base of Mount Subasio, this award-winning olive-oil mill organizes group or private tours and tastings.

🏛 Via Banche 1/B
ⓦ frantoiodispello.it

La Bottega di Teresa Prodotti Tipici Umbri
This gorgeous store stocks a plethora of Umbrian-made groceries, including cured meats and cheese.

🏛 Via Garibaldi 1
📞 3345 871 061

A charming medieval alley with views of the countryside, Spello

Todi's central town square, the beautiful Piazza del Popolo

4

TODI

 C5 40 km (25 miles) E of Orvieto FCU Perugia-Terni line Umbria Mobilità n Piazza del Popolo 29; 0758 956 227

First built on land occupied by the Umbri, Todi was later appropriated by the Etruscans and then the Romans. Under the latter, Todi's two hilltops were levelled out to make the splendid Piazza del Popolo. The town expanded during the Middle Ages and eventually became a papal possession. Today, Todi retains its medieval charm and stunning hilltop position.

① Piazza del Popolo

The centre of the town is, as it was in Roman times, Piazza del Popolo. This magnificent square contains the duomo, as well as three fine monuments: Palazzo del Popolo, Palazzo del Capitano and Palazzo dei Priori. This largely medieval square was chosen

> **Palazzo dei Priori has housed the city's various rulers, including the leaders of the medieval commune and the papal governors.**

as the starting point for excavations which have made it possible to reconstruct the layout of the ancient town.

---

② Palazzo dei Priori

 Piazza del Popolo 0758 944148 To the public

This palace, situated on the southern side of Piazza del Popolo, was built between 1293 and 1385. At the top left of the façade is an eagle in bronze, the symbol of the town and the work of Giovanni di Gigliaccio in 1339. According to tradition, the original Umbrian town was built where an eagle had dropped a table-

HIDDEN GEM
Post Office Frescoes

A short walk from Palazzo dei Priori is a beautiful post office, featuring pointed arches and a fresco by Andrea Polinori, the most important 17th-century painter in Todi.

cloth taken from a local family. Over the centuries the palazzo has housed the city's various rulers, including the leaders of the medieval commune and the papal governors.

---

③   Palazzo del Capitano and Palazzo del Popolo

 Piazza del Popolo

Palazzo del Capitano dates from the late 13th century. Its façade has mullioned Gothic windows and a grand arched staircase which serves both the Palazzo del Capitano and the adjacent Palazzo del Popolo. Sala del Capitano, with remains of frescoes, medieval coats of arms and a 14th-century *Crucifixion*, can also be accessed from here. Palazzo del Capitano houses the Museo della Città (Civic Museum) as well, which chronicles the 1,000-year history of the town of Todi. The palazzo is connected to the Palazzo del Popolo by a 17th-century overpass, which was refurbished in 1997.

Palazzo del Popolo is one of the oldest buildings of its type in Italy. Built in Lombard-Gothic form, the palace features lovely swallowtail crenellations (a Guelf motif). Here, visitors will find the **Museo Pinacoteca**, which has a decent archaeological collection; the Museo Etrusco-Romano; and some impressive paintings, of which the most significant is a *Coronation of the Virgin* (1507–11) by Giovanni di Pietro, known as Spagna.

Museo Pinacoteca

☎ 0758 944 148 ⏰ Apr-Oct: 10am-1:30pm & 3-6pm Tue-Sun & hols; Nov-Mar: 10:30am-1pm & 2:30-5pm Tue-Sun & hols ⏳ 25 Dec

④

Duomo

🏛 Piazza del Popolo
☎ 0758 943 041
⏰ 8am-dusk daily

Dedicated to Maria Santissima Annunziata, the duomo was founded in the 12th century, probably on the site of a Roman temple, but wasn't completed for another 200 years. The Romanesque façade is divided horizontally by cornices. An 18th-century flight of steps leads up to a carved 16th-century door, above which is a beautiful rose window (1515). Pilaster strips, small loggias and mullioned windows adorn the right-hand side and the tall apse.

Inside, the church has a beamed roof and splendid Gothic capitals, as well as a superb 16th-century choir. The central space and the chapels contain various works of art, the most interesting of which are near the altar: two paintings by Spagna and a painted wooden crucifix from the 13th and 14th centuries. There is also a crypt, which contains three figures originally on the façade, and a handful of Roman remains.

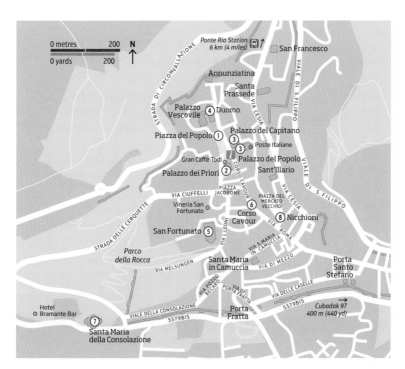

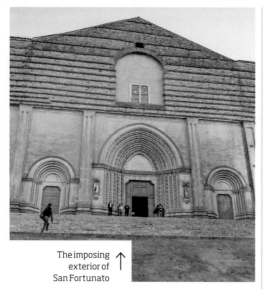

The imposing ↑
exterior of
San Fortunato

⑤

San Fortunato

 Piazza Umberto I ⏱ **Oct-Mar: 10am-1pm daily (Mon-Thu: by appt); Apr-Sep: 10am-1pm & 3-6pm Mon-Fri, 10am-6pm Sat & Sun** ⏱ **25 Dec**

The enormous hilltop church of San Fortunato is one of Todi's most spectacular sights. Commissioned by the bishop of Todi, Matteo d'Acquasparta, it was built in two phases: the first from 1292–1328 and the second in the 1400s.

The building's unfinished façade, which is a mixture of Romanesque and Gothic styles, stands out at the

---

🔺 GREAT VIEW
Stunning Skyline

Inside San Fortunato is a spiral staircase that leads to a tall bell tower, the Campanile di San Fortunato. There are beautiful views of the town's terracotta roofs and the surrounding countryside from here.

---

top of an imposing flight of steps. It has a campanile with splendid views open to the public.

Through the fine Gothic central doorway lies a wonderfully airy Gothic interior, which does not follow the traditional Franciscan model. It is a rare example in Italy of a Gothic hall church; that is, in which the two side aisles are as high as (though much narrower than) the nave. Note the lovely and unusual ribbed cross vaults, the fine late 16th-century choir stalls, the raised chapels along the sides, and the Gothic baptismal font.

Frescoes decorate many of the chapels and include, in the fifth chapel on the left, some scenes from the *Life of St John the Baptist* by the Giotto school, and, in the fourth chapel on the right, a *Madonna and Child* (1432) by Masolino da Panicale.

The church is also famous for the tomb of Jacopone da Todi, in the crypt beneath the altar. Jacopone was a rich merchant who, following the death of his devout wife, Vanna, became a mystic and a poet. His devotion was reputedly so

extreme that he was rejected even by the Franciscans. He was accused of heresy on a number of occasions and is mainly remembered for his *Laudi*, one of the fundamental texts in the birth of Italian literature. A local of Todi, he died in 1306 and gradually became the symbol of the medieval town. He is still the best-known figure in the cultural history of Todi.

Extending westwards from San Fortunato is a large public park, where a fortress commissioned by Cardinal Albornoz stood until 1503.

---

⑥

Corso Cavour

Descending the steps of Via San Fortunato brings you to the steep Corso Cavour, the "Rua degli Speziali" (spice sellers' street) of medieval Todi. Halfway along is a fountain known as the Fonte Rua (1606), or Fonte Cesia (after the bishop who had it built), and, at the end, Porta Marzia, a medieval arch made out of material salvaged from other buildings.

---

⑦

Santa Maria della Consolazione

 Viale della Consolazione ⏱ **Apr-Jun, Sep & Oct: 9am-12:30pm & 3-6:30pm Wed-Mon & hols; Jul & Aug: 9:30am-12:30pm & 3:30-6:30pm Wed-Mon & hols; Nov-Mar: 9:30am-12:30pm & 2:30-5pm Wed-Mon & hols**

This church, located outside the city walls, is one of the masterpieces of the Umbrian Renaissance. Begun in 1508 and finished in 1607, it has been attributed by some to Bramante, one of the architects of St Peter's in Rome. In fact, there is no documentary evidence of any such project by the great architect, though it is just possible that

Cola di Caprarola, who started the project, may have used drawings by Bramante.

The distinctive silhouette of the church – familiar from the covers of dozens of publications devoted to Todi – is built on a square plan and rises to a great dome. Encircling the main structure are four apses, of which one, to the north, is semicircular and three are polygonal; they have two orders of pilasters, with a mixture of capitals, and are pierced by elegant windows. The drum which supports the great dome is narrower than the main body of the church, leaving space for a raised terrace, guarded by four eagles sculpted by Antonio Rosignoli in the 17th century. The views from here are great. The Baroque doorways date from the 18th and 19th centuries.

The airy and light interior, in the form of a Greek cross, is also Baroque and contains statues of the apostles. In the apse is the venerated fresco of the *Madonna della Consolazione* (15th century). The church was built to protect the fresco.

---

 ⑧

Nicchioni

🏛 Piazza del Mercato Vecchio

Walk through Porta Marzia, and turn left into Via Mercato Vecchio. At the end of Via Mercato Vecchio, the old medieval market square (Piazza del Mercato) is dominated by four Roman arches, the so-called Nicchioni (niches). These most probably date from the Augustan era, and either supported a raised street or formed part of the wall of a Roman basilica.

→
Santa Maria della Consolazione, a feat of architecture and a Todi landmark

DRINK

Gran Caffè Tod

This welcoming café stands out for its frothy cappuccinos and giant arcade machine.

🏛 Piazza del Popolo 47
📞 0758 944 611

Hotel Bramante Bar

The bar at this elegant hotel serves curated cocktails and wines. The outdoor terrace has incredible views.

🏛 Via Circonvallazione Orvietana Est 48
📞 0758 948 381

Cubadak 97

This brewery offers a wonderful selection of beers and wines, plus a tasty pub menu.

🏛 Via del Crocefisso 4-6
📞 3456 018 583

Vineria San Fortunato

The lovely terrace of this classic *enoteca* is the highlight.

🏛 Piazza Umberto 5
📞 0753 721 180

5

ORVIETO

🅰B5 🚗40 km (25 miles) W of Todi 🚆Milan-Rome
line 🚌 ℹ️Piazza del Duomo 24, 0763 341 772;
www.orvietoviva.com

A city called Velzna in the Etruscan era, Orvieto was
taken over by the Romans in 264 BCE, who virtually
destroyed it. Revival came only in the Middle Ages,
when Orvieto developed into a free and powerful
commune. Today, the old city attracts thousands of
visitors every year, who come for its medieval charm
and superb duomo.

①

Museo Archeologico
Nazionale

🏛Piazza del Duomo 📞0763
341 039 🕐8:30am-7:30pm
Tue-Fri 🚫1 Jan, 1 May, 25 Dec

On the scenic Piazza del
Duomo, next to the imposing
mass of the cathedral, stands
the Palazzo Papale, which
includes three 14th-century
buildings, commissioned by
popes Urban IV, Gregory X and
Martin IV and later combined
into one complex.

The Museo Archeologico
Nazionale, housed in the
Palazzo del Martino IV, has
a particularly fine Etruscan
collection, including bronzes
and mirrors. Several tombs
and funerary objects are
among the exhibits, including
frescoes from 2nd-century-
BCE tombs and two
painted 4th-century CE
tombs from Settecamini.

②

Palazzo Soliano and
Museo Emilio Greco

🏛Piazza del Duomo
🕐Hours vary, check
website 🌐museomodo.it

Commissioned in 1297
by Pope Boniface VIII, this
austere building was not
completed until 1359.
In the early days, it was
used as a storehouse by
the Fabbrica del Duomo
(cathedral works). Later,
from the mid-16th century
onwards, the hall on the
ground floor was used
by Orvieto's stonemasons.
The structure is very simple,
consisting of two large
rooms, one on top of the
other. The lower room
has a line of pilasters
and arches and opens
out into a grand, monu-
mental staircase.

Palazzo Soliano houses
a substantial collection
of 20th-century sculptures,
drawings and lithographs
given to the city by Emilio
Greco, a contemporary
Sicilian artist.

③

Museo dell'Opera
del Duomo

🏛Piazza del Duomo
📞0763 343 592 🕐Apr-Sep:
9:30am-7pm daily; Mar &
Oct: 9:30am-6pm Mon-Sat,
1-5:30pm Sun (Nov-Feb: to
5pm Mon-Sat & 4:30pm Sun)

The Palazzo Papale also
houses a fascinating museum

↑ Looking towards hilltop Orvieto, and *(inset)* a charming cobbled alley

dedicated to the cathedral. Exhibits include paintings, statues and various other works of art that once filled the cathedral, dating from the Middle Ages up to the 18th century. Among them are paintings by Italian painter Simone Martini, a series of large statues formerly in the cathedral and also a collection of church ornaments.

(4)

Orvieto Underground

🏛 Tours start from the Piazza Duomo 23 🕚 11am, 12:15pm, 4pm & 5:15pm (book in advance) 🌐 orvieto underground.it

Beneath Orvieto is a system of caves, wells, tunnels and chambers, which date from the Etruscan era to the Middle Ages. This subterranean city was discovered by a group of speleologists following a landslide in 1980. It is believed that the precarious and porous nature of the tufa material (so soft it can be scratched away) led the ancient inhabitants to burrow

TOP 3 UNDERGROUND SIGHTS

Pozzo della Cava
🏛 Via della Cava 28
🌐 pozzodellacava.it
This site has medieval pottery kilns and hand-dug Etruscan wells.

Sant'Andrea
The basement of this church *(p127)* is home to historic artifacts.

Hadrian's Labyrinth
🏛 Via della Pace 26
🌐 labirintodiadriano.com
Etruscan wells, tunnels and cisterns are located under a pastry shop.

beneath "la Rupe" (The Rock), a volcanic plateau that has been supporting the city for almost 3,000 years. Here, they created an artificial underground industrial complex, which included an olive-oil mill, pottery kilns, cisterns, mangers and troughs for labouring animals, and nest holes to raise doves and pigeons.

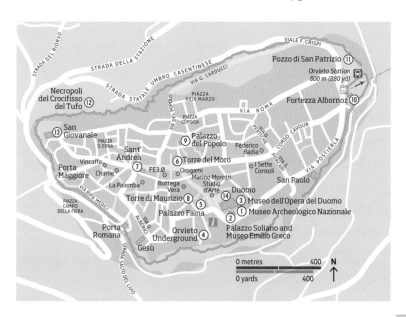

SHOP

Marino Moretti Studio d'Arte

A world-renowned ceramicist showcases his extraordinary majolica pottery at this tiny gallery across from the cathedral.

⌂ Via del Duomo 55
🌐 marinomoretti.it

Orogami

At this store, gold- and silversmiths Massimo and Tiziana hand design exquisite jewellery and wearable art inspired by Orvieto's artifacts and architecture.

⌂ Via del Duomo 14/16
🌐 orogami.com

Federico Badia

This bottega handcrafts bespoke shoes and other distinctive leather goods.

⌂ Corso Cavour 263
🌐 federicobadia shoes.com

Palazzo Faina (Museo Civico and Museo Claudio Faina)

⌂ Piazza del Duomo 29
☎ 0763 341 511
🕐 Apr-Sep: 9:30am-6pm Wed-Mon; Oct-Mar: 10am-5pm Wed-Mon

This 19th-century palazzo opposite the duomo houses two museums – the Museo Civico, on the ground floor, and the Museo Claudio Faina on the first and second floors. The palazzo has been home to the museums since 1954, when the building's last heir, Claudio Faina junior, left his wealth to the Orvieto Municipality. The Museo Civico showcases artifacts such as 5th-century terracotta and funerary slabs from the Etruscan era. The Museo Claudio Faina is an extraordinarily rich private collection gathered by the Faina counts in the 19th century. Among the exhibits are beautiful Etruscan vases, superb jewellery from the 5th century BCE onwards, a collection of coins and a series of exquisite Attic vases. There is a wonderful view of the duomo from the top floor.

← Red-figure pottery *Pelike*, Museo Claudio Faina

↑ Torre del Moro seen from a narrow alley in the old town

Torre del Moro

⌂ Corso Cavour 87
🕐 Mar, Apr, Sep & Oct: 10am-7pm; May-Aug: 10am-8pm; Nov-Feb: 10:30am-4:30pm daily
🌐 coopcarli.it

The 13th-century "Tower of the Moor" rises 42 m (137 ft) above Corso Cavour, Orvieto's main street, where it meets Via del Duomo. It owes its name to the figure on the coat of arms of the Pucci, a local family. Its 14th-century bell is still in working order. Visitors can climb 248 steps to the top of the tower to enjoy 360-degree views of the city and the surrounding countryside.

Alongside the tower is the Palazzo dei Sette (1300), built as the seat of the seven (*sette*) magistrates in charge of the commune, and later the seat of the papal governor.

---

⑦
Sant'Andrea

 Piazza della Repubblica

This church is one of the oldest buildings in Orvieto. Founded in the 7th century, Sant'Andrea was built upon walls of probable Etruscan origin, over which a Roman temple was later built. It was then rebuilt in stages during the 12th–14th centuries. Sant'Andrea was the most important church in Orvieto. It was here that Pope Innocent III proclaimed the Fourth Crusade in 1201 and that Martin IV was crowned pope in 1281, in the presence of Charles of Anjou. Important elements include the Gothic door, by Marco da Siena, designed by Maestro Vetrino (1487), and the imposing 12-sided bell tower, with three orders of two-mullioned windows

and a series of coats of arms, placed here when restoration was undertaken in 1920–30. The interior is supported by great granite columns, probably Roman, and is decorated with fragments of frescoes and a 10th-century pulpit.

---

⑧
Torre di Maurizio

 Via del Duomo

At the corner of Via del Duomo and the cathedral square is a mercurial clock tower built between 1347 and 1348. Made to mark the daily work shifts of the cathedral workers, it is the oldest mechanical, self-propelled timepiece of its kind in operation today. Atop the tower is a bronze statue of a jacquemart, hammer in hand, which is connected to a chronometer below. At the stroke of each hour, the figure strikes the bell, as it has for centuries.

⑨
Palazzo del Popolo

 Piazza del Popolo
To the public

The heart of the city in ancient times, the Piazza del Popolo is home to the Palazzo del Popolo, first described in the city records at the end of the 13th century. Built from the local tufa stone and topped by a bell tower, it is an important example of Orvieto civic architecture from the late 13th century. Ornamentations include an external staircase, an open loggia, crenellations, and mullioned windows linked by a cornice. The palazzo is now a conference centre.

↓ Nave of the church of Sant'Andrea featuring tall granite columns

Fortezza Albornoz

🏠 Via Postierla ⏰ Daily

Dominating the eastern end of Orvieto is the Fortezza (fort), built by Cardinal Albornoz in 1364 to bolster the power of the papacy. The locals destroyed it soon afterwards, and not much remains today. However, the fortress is an excellent vantage point from which to enjoy superb views over the city and the plain, as well as being a tranquil spot, surrounded by several gardens.

A short distance away on the south side of the tufa cliff is the Necropoli della Cannicella, an Etruscan burial site dating from the 7th–3rd centuries BCE. A further 3 km (2 miles) south, just off SS71, is the Abbazia di Santi Severo e Martirio, a great medieval monastery complex. Now partly converted into a hotel, the monastery belonged to the Benedictines until 1221 and then the Premonstratensians (a French Order founded in 1120 by St Norbert).

There is much that dates from the original construction (12th–13th centuries). The splendid 12-sided Romanesque tower dates from the 12th century and a church, reached through a great 13th-century arch, features a single nave with a ribbed vault, an inlaid marble floor in the Cosmatesque style and several fragments of medieval frescoes. The barrel-vaulted Oratorio del Crocifisso, once the monks' refectory, is adorned with a 13th-century fresco depicting the *Crucifixion with Saints*. Also of interest is the 13th-century Abbot's House.

---

⑪ Pozzo di San Patrizio

🏠 Viale Sangallo
📞 0763 343 768 ⏰ Jan, Feb, Nov & Dec: 10am–4:45pm daily; Mar, Apr & Sep: 9am–6:45pm daily; May–Aug: 9am–8pm daily

Located at the eastern end of Corso Cavour, at Piazza Cahen, the Pozzo di San Patrizio is one of Orvieto's best-known monuments. Commissioned in 1527 by Pope Clement VII and designed by Antonio da Sangallo the Younger, the 62-m (203-ft) well is a superb piece of engineering. Crucial to the design are two 248-step spiral staircases: one was used for the descent and one for the ascent, so that donkeys carrying pitchers of water would not meet on the way. The stairways are lit by 72 windows.

---

⑫ Necropoli del Crocifisso del Tufo

🏠 Strada di Stazione
⏰ 9am–7pm Wed & Fri, 9am–3pm Thu & Sat, 1–7pm Sun
🚫 Last Sun of each month

Around 1.5 km (1 mile) north of Orvieto, at the foot of

One of the spiral staircases in the Pozzo di San Patrizio and *(inset)* its exterior ↓

↑ Stone façade of the Temple of Belvedere, Necropoli del Crocifisso del Tufo

the tufa cliff, is the Necropoli del Crocifisso del Tufo. It can be accessed on foot via a ramp located near the car park at Porta Vivaria.

This Etruscan cemetery complex dates from the 6th–3rd centuries BCE and consists of small chambered tombs built of tufa blocks. It features a stone bench for laying out the corpse. On the lintel over the entrance to each tomb is the name of the person or family buried there. The site seems to have an essentially "urban" layout, following what would be defined today as a town plan.

It was discovered only in the 19th century, by foreign archaeologists who passed on some of the finds to the Louvre and the British Museum. It wasn't until 1880 that the site was first explored in a scientific, nonintrusive

way and finally began to pique the interest of the Italian authorities. Over 200 tombs have now been found. The majority of the important funerary objects discovered in the tombs are now distributed among Orvieto's museums.

San Giovanale

🏠 **Via Volsinia**

The oldest still-existing church in Umbria, Chiesa di San Giovanale is located at the northwest edge of a cliff in Orvieto's old medieval quarter. Built atop the remains of both an earlier Christian church and an even earlier ancient Etruscan temple likely dedicated to Jupiter, it was remodelled in the Baroque style in 1632. The interior is simple and austere, with one pillar wrapped in massive iron belts to support the vaults and its walls painted with votive frescoes. The latter were once obscured by white lime, which had been used to disinfect the church during the plague, but were recovered during a recent renovation.

> **The oldest still-existing church in Umbria, Chiesa di San Giovanale is located at the northwest edge of a cliff in Orvieto's old medieval quarter.**

EAT

La Palomba
Try *tartufo umbrichelli* (black truffles shaved over a pasta) here.

🏠 Via Cipriano Menente 16 📞 0763 343 395

€€€

Charlie
This pizzeria plus trattoria has a pretty outdoor garden.

🏠 Via Loggia dei Mercanti 14 📞 0763 344 766

€€€

I Sette Consoli
This award-winning, fine-dining establishment is hard to beat.

🏠 Piazza Sant'Angelo 1A 🌐 isetteconsoli.it

€€€

DRINK

Bottega Vera
This cute wine bar has pavement-side bistro tables.

🏠 Via del Duomo 36/38 🌐 bottegaveraorvieto.it

FE3.Ø
Set on a pretty street, this chic pub is the only microbrewery in Orvieto.

🏠 Via Gualverio Michelangeli 7 📞 3374 563 160

Vincaffe
Grab a seat at the wooden bar of this cosy *enoteca*, offering regional varietals.

🏠 Via Filippeschi 39 📞 0763 340 099

(14) 🚆

DUOMO

🏛 Piazza del Duomo 🕐 Duomo and chapel: Apr-Sep: 9:30am-7pm daily; Oct-Mar: 9:30am-6pm Mon-Sat, 1-4:30pm Sun (Mar & Oct: to 4:30pm Sun) 🌐 opsm.it

Towering over a square-shaped piazza, this majestic basilica is dedicated to the Assumption of the Virgin Mary. It is considered one of the greatest artistic and architectural achievements of the Middle Ages, thanks to its striking striped façade, glittering mosaics and elegant rose window and frescoes.

Orvieto's magnificent Duomo, which dominates the skyline, was founded by Pope Nicholas IV in 1290. Things got off to a bad start and, in 1308, the Sienese architect and sculptor, Lorenzo Maitani, was brought in to save the building. It wasn't finished for another 300 years. Maitani himself was largely responsible for the 52-m (170-ft) façade, which has his own magnificently detailed bas-reliefs of scenes from the Old and New Testaments, a superb rose window, 16th-century statues and multi-coloured mosaics (not original). The striped design outside is carried through into the Romanesque nave, which has alabaster windows and is divided by columns with elaborate capitals. Inside, the masterpiece is the chapel of the Madonna di San Brizio, with frescoes by Fra Angelico and Luca Signorelli and portraits of famous poets such as Dante.

FRESCOES BY LUCA SIGNORELLI

A fascinating cycle of frescoes narrating events related to the apocalypse unfolds on the walls of the Cappella della Madonna di San Brizio. Signorelli tackles the themes of the Last Judgment - *The Day of Judgment, The Preaching of the Antichrist, The Resurrection of the Dead, The Damned Consigned to Hell, The Blessed Entering Heaven* and *Angels Guide the Elect to Paradise*. The three-dimensionality and energy emanating from the figures heighten the drama and precede the work of Michelangelo in the Sistine Chapel.

The sanctuary walls feature 14th-century frescoes by Ugolino di Prete Ilario.

Among the stained glass in the apse is the Nativity by Giovanni Bonino di Assisi.

The Cappella del Corporale has superb 14th-century paintings and frescoes.

The Reliquario del Corporale contains the altar cloth associated with the Miracle of Bolsena.

Illustration of the Romanesque-style Duomo of Orvieto ↑

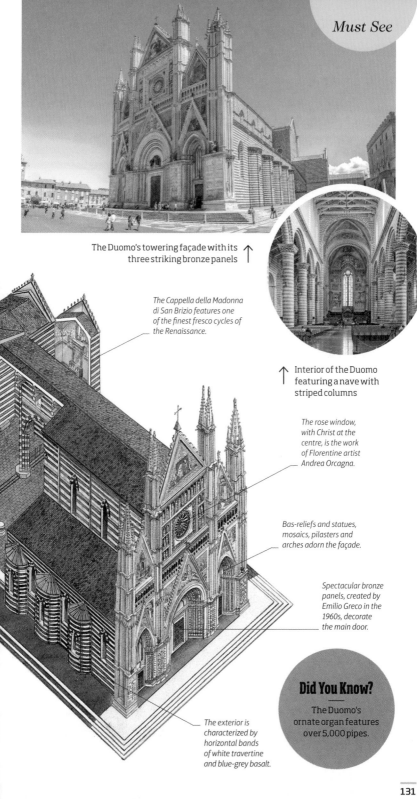

The Duomo's towering façade with its three striking bronze panels ↑

The Cappella della Madonna di San Brizio features one of the finest fresco cycles of the Renaissance.

↑ Interior of the Duomo featuring a nave with striped columns

The rose window, with Christ at the centre, is the work of Florentine artist Andrea Orcagna.

Bas-reliefs and statues, mosaics, pilasters and arches adorn the façade.

Spectacular bronze panels, created by Emilio Greco in the 1960s, decorate the main door.

Did You Know?

The Duomo's ornate organ features over 5,000 pipes.

The exterior is characterized by horizontal bands of white travertine and blue-grey basalt.

EXPERIENCE MORE

 6

Allerona

A5 ⏱18 km (11 miles) NW of Orvieto Ⓦ comune. allerona.tr.it

Perched atop a rocky spur and surrounded by forests of beech and oak, Allerona is one of the prettiest hilltop hamlets in Umbria. It consists of a network of charming cobbled streets lined by old stone buildings. Likely beginning life as an early Etruscan settlement, the village became the site of a feudal castle, built by the Monaldeschi family, in the Middle Ages. The building was destroyed in 1495 and

 INSIDER TIP
Village Life

Run by a local family, Villaggio Tours *(www. villaggiotours.com)* offers week-long stays in Allerona. It includes olive-picking sessions, cooking classes and excursions to Orvieto *(p124)* and Lazio.

today, only the medieval walls remain, which can be accessed via two stone gateways (the Porta del Sole and Porta della Luna). Other historic sights include the 17th-century church of the Madonna dell'Acqua; a diminutive octagonal temple built over a 15th-century chapel; and the remains of a Roman aqueduct, located just outside the hamlet.

7

Parco Fluviale del Tevere

🅰C5-C6 🅝W of Todi 🚉Orvieto, Milan-Rome line; Todi, FCU Perugia-Terni line 🚌 🅸Piazza del Comune 1, Baschi; www.parks.it

This verdant river park extends for some 7,295 ha (18,025 acres) from the bridge of Montemolino, at the gates of Todi, south as far as Lago di Alviano, and has great wildlife and lovely scenery. It includes around 50 km (31 miles) of land along the banks of the Tiber River and two artificial

> Allerona is one of the prettiest hilltop hamlets in Umbria. It consists of a network of charming cobbled streets lined by old stone buildings.

lakes (Alviano and Corbara). The main access to the park is at the medieval hilltown of Baschi, close to the junction of the S448 and the motorway. The River Tiber, one moment placid and the next turbulent, is home to a variety of birds, among them blue heron and kingfishers, as well as fresh-water fish. Poplars, alders and willows, typical riverside vegetation, cloak the sides.

Steep valleys sweep away from the river and extend as far as the Apennines: the wildest is the Gole del Forello, considered one of the most interesting biotopes in the region. On the northern banks of Lago di Corbara, not far from the fortified village of Prodo, winds the Gole di Prodo, a deep gorge best suited to experienced and well-equipped hikers and mountain climbers. Numerous birds of prey, including buzzards, sparrowhawks and kites, can

be seen in these remote areas, where the vegetation consists mainly of trees such as holm oaks and hornbeams, and shrubs such as broom and heather. The marshes in the Lago di Alviano basin, with their own particular bird-life and plants, are also of great interest.

Besides the natural beauty and the opportunities for outdoor sports, the park also incorporates sites of historical and archaeological interest. Digs are under way in various spots, including in the Vallone di San Lorenzo (site of several necropolises) and in the area of the ancient river port of Pagliano, at the confluence of the Paglia and Tiber rivers; the port's existence confirms the importance of the Tiber as a communication route of the central Italic peoples.

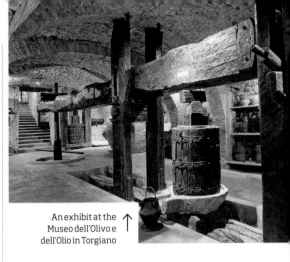

An exhibit at the Museo dell'Olivo e dell'Olio in Torgiano ↑

 8

Torgiano

🅰C4 🚇21 km (13 miles) W of Assisi 🚉Perugia and Assisi stations, Foligno-Terontola line 🚌 🛈Corso Vittorio Emanuele 25; 0756 211682

The small town of Torgiano occupies a lovely position at the confluence of the Tiber and Chiascio rivers. Inhabited since the Roman era, it was rebuilt during the Middle Ages as a fortified site to guard the territory of Perugia – as the 13th-century Torre Baglioni still bears witness.

Torgiano's agricultural roots and long-standing wine practices are acknowledged in the town's coat of arms and recorded in the excellent **Museo del Vino and Osteria**. Housed in the 17th-century

 ←

Tranquil Lago di Corbara, found within the Parco Fluviale del Tevere

Palazzo Baglioni, this is a private museum owned by the Lungarotti family, who are among the best-known wine producers in Umbria. The museum illustrates the history of oenology and vine-growing since antiquity, through a collection of tools used for the production of wine over the centuries, as well as old books and printed material relating to wine. There is also a valuable collection of majolica pieces, among them a plate by Maestro Giorgio da Gubbio (1528) and a tondo depicting Bacchus which is attributed to Girolamo della Robbia. Next door to the museum is the Osteria del Museo, where it is possible to taste and buy wines from the **Cantine Giorgio Lungarotti**.

In an additional demonstration of the high esteem in which local agricultural products are held, the Lungarotti Foundation has also set up the **Museo dell'Olivo e dell'Olio**. Displays regarding olives and olive oil are housed in restored medieval dwellings. High-quality olive oils and balsamic vinegar produced on the estate are offered for sale in the winery shop.

Museo del Vino and Osteria
 🏠Corso Vittorio Emanuele 31 🕙10am-1pm & 3-6pm daily 🆆muvit.it

Cantine Giorgio Lungarotti
📞0759 886 649 (call ahead)

Museo dell'Olivo e dell'Olio
🏠Via Garibaldi 10 🕙10am-1pm & 3-6pm daily (by appt) 🆆muvit.it

---

TOP 3 WINERIES IN CENTRAL UMBRIA

Lungarotti
🅰C4 🏠Viale Lungarotti 2, Torgiano 🆆lungarotti.it
The main cellar of Lungarotti is at Torgiano, along with fascinating wine and olive oil museums.

Scacciadiavoli
🅰D5 🏠Località Cantinone 31, Montefalco 🆆cantina scacciadiavoli.it
Founded in 1884, Scacciadiavoli is one of Montefalco's (p141) oldest wineries. Visit to see how well-known Sagrantino and other local wines are made.

Tenuta Bellafonte
🅰D4 🏠Via Colle Nottolo 2, Bevagna 🆆tenutabella fonte.it
Bellafonte offers various tours of the winery and includes accommodation, too.

↑ A maze of medieval buildings in the fortified town of Bettona

⑨
Bettona

🗺 D4 **🏛 17 km (11 miles) SW of Assisi** **🚉 Perugia and Assisi stations, Foligno-Terontola line** **🚌** **ℹ Pro Loco, Corso Marconi; www.comune. bettona.pg.it**

Around 6 km (3.5 miles) from Torgiano, this historical town is among the extremely rare centres where Etruscan culture originated. Evidence of its beginnings is clear from the huge blocks of stone set into the medieval walls. The best example is the 40-m (131-ft) section at the northwestern corner; other sections are of medieval origin, but rest on an Etruscan base. The entire circuit of the outer walls can be explored on foot.

The medieval town is home to works of art that some have attributed to the school of Perugino, while others believe they are the work of the master himself. The first is a processional banner with a *Madonna and Child and St Anne*. It was previously kept with other important works in the 13th-century church of Santa Maria Maggiore. Today, it is on display in the **Pinacoteca Comunale**, a museum housed in the Palazzo del Podestà. The museum's collection also has *St Anthony of Padua* by Perugino, *Adoration of the Shepherds* by Dono Doni (a masterpiece from 1543), and works of Jacopo Siculo, Niccolò Alunno, Tiberio d'Assisi and Fiorenzo di Lorenzo.

Pinacoteca Comunale

♿ 🏛 Palazzo del Podestà, Piazza Cavour 3 📞 0759 87347 🕐 Hours vary, call ahead 🚫 1 Jan, 25 Dec

⑩
Bevagna

🗺 D4 **🏛 11 km (7 miles) southwest of Spello** **🚉 Foligno, 9 km (6 miles), Rome-Ancona line** **🚌** **ℹ Pro Loco, Piazza Filippo Silvestri 1; 0742 361 667; www.prolocobevagna.it**

This ancient town, previously called *Mevania*, has presumably been inhabited since the 7th century BCE. The town experienced its most affluent period under the Romans. Following a period of decline during the Lombard era, it saw a revival in the 12th century; this was when Bevagna acquired its current appearance.

The main entrance to the town is from Porta Foligno, from where Corso Matteotti leads to the medieval Piazza Silvestri that features the Gothic Palazzo dei Consoli and three churches: San Silvestro, San Michele Arcangelo and Santi Domenico e Giacomo.

Corso Matteotti follows the route of the cardo – one of the main streets through the Roman settlement. In the northern part, where

the forum stood, various traces of the Roman era have been restored and some still survive, among them the ruins of a temple (now the church of the Madonna della Neve), a theatre and baths. Off Piazza Garibaldi is the 13th-century church of San Francesco. Inside are frescoes by a local artist known as Fantino.

Also worth a visit is the **Museo Civico**, which has many Roman and pre-Roman finds, as well as the fine *Ciccoli Altarpiece* (1565–70) by Dono Doni. There is also a section devoted to the local 16th- and 17th-century artists.

Museo Civico

⊛ ⌂ Corso Matteotti 70
☎ 0742 360 031 ⌚ Apr–Sep: 10:30am–6pm Fri–Sun
🚫 1 Jan, 25 Dec

---

⑪

Deruta

🅰 C4 📍 25 km (16 miles)
N of Todi 🚌 ℹ Pro Loco, Piazza dei Consoli 4; 0759 711 559

On a knoll overlooking the Tiber valley, Deruta has been inhabited

THE CERAMICS OF THE TIBER

Umbria is famed for its exquisite ceramics, with the manufacture of these items important to the local economies of many towns, especially Deruta. In fact, a vast majority of the main production centres are still found along the Tiber, thanks to a greater availability of clay and the silica needed for the glazes.

since Neolithic times, and still bears traces of its history in part of the walls and in the three arches that give access to the old centre. The town's name may derive from the fact that it has been destroyed ("*distrutta*") several times.

The heart of Deruta is Piazza dei Consoli where, as in most medieval settlements, all the chief religious and civic monuments stand: Palazzo dei Consoli, housing the town hall and the Pinacoteca (art gallery), and the Romanesque-Gothic church of San Francesco. Set in the former monastery of San Francesco, next door to the church, is the **Museo Regionale**

della Ceramica, which is one of the most important museums of its kind. It documents the production of jars, plates and other everyday items since in the Middle Ages, underlining the role of ceramics in Deruta. The town has many workshops making and selling majolica pieces. Pottery is also a highlight at the church of the **Madonna dei Bagni** (1657), 2 km (1 mile) south of Deruta. Its walls are covered in old *ex votos* made of Deruta pottery.

Museo Regionale della Ceramica

⌂ Largo San Francesco
⌚ Jun–Sep: 10am–1:30pm & 2:30–6pm daily 🌐 museo ceramicadideruta.it

Madonna dei Bagni

⌂ SS E45, exit Casalina
☎ 0759 724 232 ⌚ 8am–12:30pm & 2:30–6:30pm daily

↑ Church of San Silvestro towering over the medieval Piazza Silvestri, Bevagna

Panorama of the valley in Bettona

EAT

Serpillo

Set in an old olive-oil mill, this spot offers seasonal Italian fare.

🅐D4 🏠Via di Mezzo 1, Torre del Colle (near Bevagna)
🌐en.serpillo.com

€€€

Umami Food Boutique

Try gluten-free and organic dishes here.

🅐D4 🏠Via Giuseppe Garibaldi 11, Foligno
🌐umami-foligno. business.site

€€€

Foligno

🅐D4 🚗7 km (4 miles) S of Spello 🚆Rome-Ancona line 🚌 ℹCorso Cavour 126; 0742 354 459

The town of Foligno lies in the plain of the River Topino, which skirts its northern edge. One of the few Umbrian towns to be built on flat land, Foligno was sited at the crossroads of two important commercial routes: the Via Flaminia and the road from Perugia to Assisi.

The principal manufacturing and commercial centre in the region, with the exception perhaps of Perugia, Foligno is a lively, dynamic city. At its heart is the Piazza della Repubblica, home to the main centres of religious and civic power. These include the duomo, built and modified between 1133 and 1512 and restored to its original Romanesque form in the early 1900s. The cathedral is known for its two façades: the main

Frescoes adorning the walls of the Museo Archeologico, and *(inset)* the simple exterior of the Palazzo ↓ Trinci, Foligno

one faces the small Piazza Don Michele Faloci Pulignani, while the south front, with its richly decorated lateral façade and splendid doorway, looks onto Piazza della Repubblica.

Opposite is the Palazzo Comunale, with a Neo-Classical façade. Originally built in the 13th century, the palace was rebuilt several times and altered completely following the earthquake of 1832. It is linked to the Palazzo Orfini, which is famous because it was probably the home of the printing house of Orfini. This was among the earliest of all Italian printing houses (1470), and the first to publish a work in Italian, Dante's *Divine Comedy* (1472).

On the northwestern side of Piazza della Repubblica is the **Palazzo Trinci**, home of the Pinacoteca Comunale and the Museo Archeologico. Among many works of art in the gallery are pictures by three notable painters born in Foligno: Ottaviano Nelli, Niccolò Alunno and Pier Antonio Mezzastris.

Other sights of interest include the monastery of Sant'Anna. It was the former home of Raphael's celebrated *Madonna di Foligno*, which was removed by Napoleon's men in

→ River Clitunno's clear springs at the lush Fonti del Clitunno

1789 and is now on display in the Vatican museum in Rome. Thankfully, however, the monastery still has several other precious works of art.

Another highlight is the 15th-century Nunziatella Oratory containing several works by Perugino. Found above the right-hand altar, the *Baptism of Jesus* (1513) is the most notable and is similar to the one he painted in the Sistine Chapel.

Heading east out of Foligno along the SS77, then taking a fork to the right after about 2 km (1 mile), is a scenic road that leads up to the Abbazia di Sassovivo, surrounded by a dense forest of holm oaks. Founded in around 1000, the Benedictine abbey was an important political and cultural centre until the 15th century. It has an abbey church and a 13th-century Romanesque cloister, the finest of its kind in the region. There are 128 variegated double or spiral columns supporting 58 round arches, decorated with coloured marbles and two bands of mosaics. There's a 13th-century fresco, too. Also of note is the Loggia del Paradiso in the monastery.

Palazzo Trinci

 ⬛ Piazza della Repubblica ◐ 10am-7pm Tue-Sun ⬜ museifoligno.it

---

🔍 **HIDDEN GEM**
Rasiglia

About 19 km (11 miles) from Foligno is the tiny hamlet of Rasiglia. Often called "Umbria's Little Venice", it is cut through by crystal-line streams that are fed by the Sorgente Capovena spring.

---

13 🚶

Fonti del Clitunno

⬛ E5 ⬛ 25 km (16 miles) S of Spello 🚌 Campello sul Clitunno, Rome-Ancona line, Trevi, 10 km (6 miles), FCU Perugia-Terni line 🚌 ◐ Hours vary, check website ⬜ fontidelclitunno.it

Famous since antiquity, these springs emerge alongside the Via Flaminia, at Vene. The cool, limpid waters of this series of karst springs create a large pool with small islands, as well as a river of the same name.

The historic reputation of the springs comes from the oracular skills attributed to the god of the River Clitunno (Clitumnus, the messenger god). The oracle was often cited by poets, from Virgil to Byron. Some even say the water's main effect is to remove the urge to consume alcohol. The site owes its fortune to the fertility of the soil and the sheer abundance of water, so the Romans exploited it and created a holiday area here, using the springs to create public baths.

Numerous buildings and villas were constructed along the river banks, which have almost totally disappeared.

Did You Know?

Emperor Caligula often visited Fonti del Clitunno parkland to honour the god Clitunno.

Votive buildings include the **Tempietto**, which many experts say was built in the 4th–5th centuries CE, while others believe 7th–8th centuries, using the materials from an earlier Christian building. About 1 km (half a mile) north of the Fonti, the temple has a crypt and a room for worship. The latter is decorated with 7th-century frescoes, thought to be the oldest paintings with sacred subjects in Umbria. In 2011, the Tempietto was listed as a UNESCO World Heritage Site.

Just south of the springs is Campello sul Clitunno, whose Madonna della Bianca church has 16th-century frescoes.

Tempietto

 ⬛ Via del Tempio 1 📞 0743 275 085 ◐ Summer: 10:30am-7pm daily; winter: 11am-dusk Wed-Mon

⑭ Trevi

Ⓐ E5 ⏱ 19 km (12 miles) S of Spello ⓡ Rome–Ancona line, FCU Perugia-Terni line ▦ 🛈 Piazza Mazzini; www. treviturismo.it

The historic centre of Trevi "unwinds" in a stunning spiral around Monte Serano. Flooding from the River Clitunno forced the inhabitants of Roman Trevi to move to higher ground. Once this threat was averted, the modern city, Borgo Trevi, was free to develop on the plain, among the fields and olive groves.

The central Piazza Mazzini is home to the 14th-century Palazzo Comunale. Nearby is

---

SHOP

Il Frantoio

In a valley below Trevi, the Guidobaldi family has been cold-pressing oil traditionally since the early 1950s.

Ⓐ E5 Ⓐ Via Bastia 1, Frazione Matigge, Trevi ⓦ oliotrevi.it

Flaminio

Flaminio sells an array of locally sourced products including flavoured oils, pasta, legumes and wine vinegar.

Ⓐ E5 Ⓐ Via Bastia 1, Frazione Matigge, Trevi ⓦ olioflaminio.it

---

Cascioli Nadia

This family-run establishment uses ancient methods to create a flavourful and amber-coloured olive oil.

Ⓐ E5 Ⓐ Via la Valle 9, Frazione Bovara, Trevi ⓦ frantoiocasciolinadia.it

---

the monumental Palazzo Valentii, today a hotel, and the huge church of San Francesco. This 13th-century church, together with the adjacent **Raccolta d'Arte di San Francesco**, is the principal artistic attraction in the town. The church holds interesting works, including a fine organ from 1209. Housed in the church monastery since 1997, the Raccolta displays Trevi's most important works of art. The finest is the *Coronation of the Virgin* (1522) by Giovanni di Pietro, known as Spagna, which was commissioned by the friars of the church of San Martino.

The 12th-century cathedral of Sant'Emiliano stands at the summit of the hill. Restored in the 20th century, it still has three original apses. Next door, the **Palazzo Lucarini Contemporary** features a small permanent collection of contemporary art by Italian and international artists, as well as changing exhibitions.

Around 1.5 km (1 mile) north of Trevi, the **Tenuta San Pietro a Pettine** offers guided truffle hunting and also has an on-site restaurant. A further 1.5 km (1 mile) north-west of Trevi is the church of Santa Maria a Pietrarossa, named for the red stone (*pietra rossa*) in the presbytery. The church has an extensive portico, beneath which is a vast cycle of 15th-century votive frescoes.

Raccolta d'Arte di San Francesco

Ⓐ Largo Don Bosco 14 ⏱ Hours vary, check website ⓦ museitrevi.it

Palazzo Lucarini Contemporary

Ⓐ Via Beato Placido Riccardi, 11 ⏱ 3:30–6:30pm Fri–Sun ⓦ palazzolucarini.it

Tenuta San Pietro a Pettine

ⓦ sanpietroapettine.it

---

⑮ Altopiano di Colfiorito

Ⓐ E4 ⏱ 29 km (18 miles) E of Spello ⓡ Foligno, 24 km (15 miles), Rome–Ancona line ▦ 🛈 Via della Rinascita (Ex Casermette area); 0742 681 011

Heading east from Foligno, this upland plain reaches over 700 m (2,300 ft) above sea level. It consists of seven broad basins, once part of a lake that was drained in the 15th century. Of the original formation, a marsh called the Palude di Colfiorito remains. The 100-ha (250-acre) wetland is known for its aquatic vegetation and wildlife.

→

Rows of Sagrantino vineyards in Montefalco during autumn

Calcareous plains alternate with steep slopes, surrounded by the Apennine peaks in the fringes. These form part of the protected area, Parco Regionale di Colfiorito. Here, visitors can hike along a series of signposted routes. There are also traces of ancient human habitation called *castellieri* (pre-Roman villages) – the most visited is that of Monte Orve. The park houses the Museo Naturalistico, which documents the species of flora and fauna found in the region.

Montefalco

D5 18 km (11 miles) S of Spello Foligno, 12 km (7 miles), Rome-Ancona line Pro Loco, Via Ringhiera Umbra 25; 3490 928 521

Perched high on a hill, over the valleys of the Topino and Clitunno rivers, Montefalco offers superb views over Central Umbria, and has been nicknamed "the balcony of Umbria". It is also famous for its Sagrantino wine.

Montefalco retains some elements of Roman origin, but the atmosphere is, above all, medieval. At its centre, Piazza del Comune is enclosed within a circle of medieval walls with five gates, from which five main streets lead, in the shape of a star, to the central piazza. The main access to the town is via the 14th-century Porta Sant'Agostino, which has a tower on top.

The main square is home to a number of churches and palazzi, but the most important monument in the town – and one of the most famous in the region – is the former 14th-century church of **San Francesco**. The attached monastery houses the **Museo Comunale**. The highlight of this church are the frescoes painted by Benozzo Gozzoli (1420–97), a pupil of Fra Angelico and famous above all for his exquisite frescoes in the Palazzo Medici in Florence. Gozzoli's frescoes in San Francesco are found in the Cappella di San Girolamo and, more importantly, in the central apse, where the magnificent *Life of St Francis* (1452) is the most important pictorial cycle dedicated to the saint after the one in the Basilica di San Francesco in Assisi *(p108)*. The museum also contains artifacts and artworks salvaged from other local churches.

Outside the town's old walls is the convent and church of Santa Chiara. Of particular note is its chapel which is completely covered in 14th-century frescoes by Umbrian artists, narrating the lives of the saints Chiara, Caterina (Catherine) and Biagio (Blaise), and of the Virgin. On the wall of the altar a *Calvary* includes more than 45 figures.

The Franciscan convent of San Fortunato, about 1 km (half a mile) south of the town, has frescoes by Benozzo Gozzoli (1449) in the church.

San Francesco and Museo Comunale

◈ Via Ringhiera Umbra 6 0742 379 598 Hours vary, call ahead

> **Perched high on a hill, over the valleys of the Topino and Clitunno rivers, Montefalco offers superb views over Central Umbria, and has been nicknamed "the balcony of Umbria".**

A CYCLING TOUR
ASSISI-SPOLETO BIKE LANE

Assisi-Spoleto Bike Lane

CENTRAL UMBRIA

Locator Map

Length 51 km (32 miles) **Stopping-off points** Bevagna **Nearest station** Assisi railway station (Foligno-Terontola line), then take Bus E006 to the starting point **Information** www.umbriatourism.it

This cycling route was established in 1926 to connect the historic towns of the Umbrian Valley. It ventures through pretty pastoral landscapes, including swathes of sheep-speckled farmland, which are cut through by tinkling streams and rushing rivers, and surrounded by forested green hills. The route also passes through a number of picturesque towns, including the old Roman village of Cannara and Bevagna, a medieval hilltown.

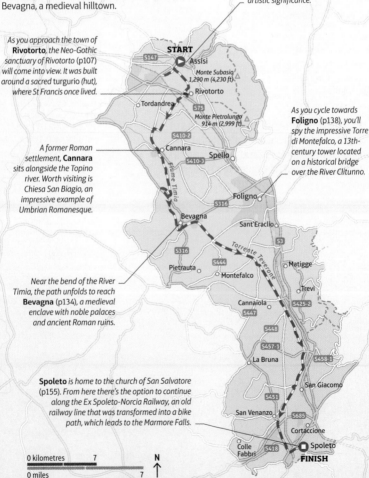

Known as the birthplace of St Francis, hilltop **Assisi** offers breathtaking glimpses of the Umbrian countryside, and is characterized by places of Franciscan religious and artistic significance.

As you approach the town of **Rivotorto**, the Neo-Gothic sanctuary of Rivotorto (p107) will come into view. It was built around a sacred turgurio (hut), where St Francis once lived.

As you cycle towards **Foligno** (p138), you'll spy the impressive Torre di Montefalco, a 13th-century tower located on a historical bridge over the River Clitunno.

A former Roman settlement, **Cannara** sits alongside the Topino river. Worth visiting is Chiesa San Biagio, an impressive example of Umbrian Romanesque.

Near the bend of the River Timia, the path unfolds to reach **Bevagna** (p134), a medieval enclave with noble palaces and ancient Roman ruins.

Spoleto is home to the church of San Salvatore (p155). From here there's the option to continue along the Ex Spoleto-Norcia Railway, an old railway line that was transformed into a bike path, which leads to the Marmore Falls.

START
Assisi
Monte Subasio 1,290 m (4,230 ft)
Rivotorto
Tordandrea
Monte Pietrolungo 914 m (2,999 ft)
S147
S75
Cannara
Spello
S410-2
S410-3
Fiume Timia
Foligno
S316
Bevagna
Sant'Eraclio
S316
S3
Pietrauta
S444
Montefalco
Matigge
Torrente Teverone
Trevi
Cannaiola
S425-2
S447
S448
S457-1
La Bruna
S458-1
San Giacomo
S451
San Venanzo
S685
Cortaccione
Colle Fabbri
S418
Spoleto
FINISH

0 kilometres 7
0 miles 7
N ↑

Cycling on the scenic
Ex Spoleto-Norcia Railway
bike path in Spoleto ↑

SOUTHERN UMBRIA

The Umbri established a number of settlements in this hilly area, including Narni and Spoleto around the 7th century BCE. As with many towns across Umbria, these were captured by the Romans following their arrival in the 4th century BCE and were later expanded in size. The Romans also set up their own settlements on the Via Flaminia – including Carsulae in the 3rd century BCE, which gradually transformed from a staging post into a bustling town – and built an impressive artificial waterfall near Terni.

During the 6th century CE, following the fall of the Roman Empire, the Lombards gained control over the area, bringing old Roman towns like Cascia and Spoleto under its rule, with the latter becoming the seat of a Lombard dukedom. Alongside the rest of Umbria, this area fell under papal control from the 12th century, with a huge fortress built in Spoleto during the 14th century, as a way to assert the authority of the papacy over both the city and the region. Terni, meanwhile, developed into a key industrial centre for mining and manufacturing. It kept this role for centuries, with the city a major site of heavy industry during the 19th and 20th centuries. Such industrial importance made it a target for bombardment by Allied forces during World War II – today, it looks modern compared with most other Umbrian towns.

Nowadays, while Southern Umbria is quieter than the rest of the region, it is becoming ever more popular thanks to its verdant national parks, Roman ruins and beautiful hilltop towns like Norcia, famous for its delicious cured meats.

SOUTHERN UMBRIA

Must Sees

1. Parco Nazionale dei Monti Sibillini
2. Spoleto
3. Terni
4. Parco Fluviale del Nera

Experience More

5. Cascia
6. Norcia
7. Narni
8. San Pietro in Valle
9. Carsulae
10. Acquasparta
11. San Gemini
12. Amelia
13. Lugnano in Teverina
14. Santa Pudenziana

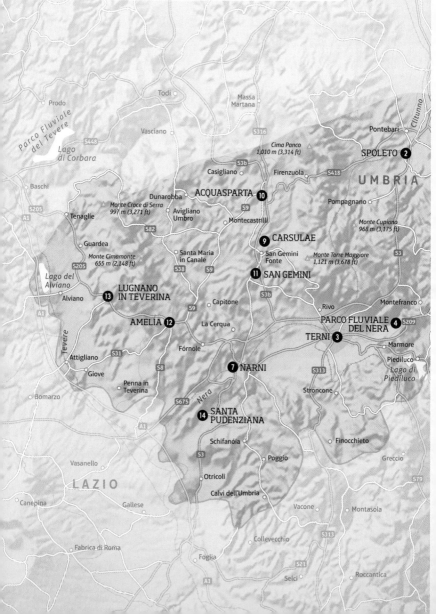

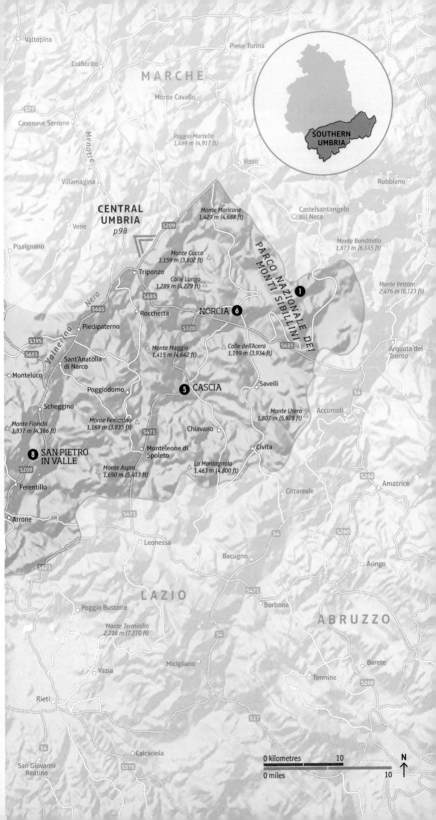

❶

PARCO NAZIONALE DEI MONTI SIBILLINI

🅰F5 🅰40 km (25 miles) E of Spoleto 🚌 🚹Info points: Amadola, Fiastra, Montefortino & Preci; www.sibillini.net

Crossing the border between Umbria and Le Marche, the Parco Nazionale dei Monti Sibillini offers a compelling combination of nature, history and legend. It provides the region's most epic scenery, including rugged peaks and tranquil lakes, as well as medieval abbeys and ancient settlements.

This national park is named after Monte Sibilla, which in turn takes its name from the legend that the mythical sibyl (*sibilla*) – prophetesses who were capable of predicting the future – once lived in a grotto on its slopes. The tallest mountain in the park, however, is the 2,476-m (8,121-ft) Monte Vettore. Its summit can be reached via a rocky hiking trail; from the top, there are fine views over the entire massif, with the dark waters of Lago di Pilato below.

Other trails cover the entire park and are suitable for both walkers and mountain bikers. The upland plains are popular for hang-gliding, and in winter the snow-covered mountains draw skiers. Drivers, meanwhile, can follow hairpin roads to some of Italy's most magical landscapes. Chief of these is the Piano Grande, an upland plain surrounded by an amphitheatre of mountains and watched over by the tiny hilltop hamlet of Castelluccio di Norcia. From late May to July, the meadow here is carpeted in the *fioritura*, an abundance of wildflowers, including poppies, cornflowers, daisies and wild mustard.

Historic sights dot the park, too, including the Abbazia di Sant'Eutizio. This abbey dates from the late 12th century, but the area drew hermits from the 6th century onwards.

STAY

Camping Sibilla
Pitch a tent or park a caravan at this campsite, which has all the comforts of home, including laundry, showers and Wi-Fi.

🅰 Via Tenna 3, Montefortino
🆆campingsibilla.it

Camping Vettore
Nestled among the mountains, this wooded campground is open year-round.

🅰Strada San Nicola 15, Balzo di Montegallo
🆆campingvettore.it

A road winding through the park's verdant hills ↑

↑ Hiking on one of the park's scenic trails, with green peaks in the distance

→ A red fox (Vulpes vulpes), one of many wildlife species that inhabit the park

WILDLIFE IN THE MONTI SIBILLINI

The park is an ideal habitat for many different species. The wolf and wildcat are present in small numbers, but there are healthy populations of red fox, roe deer, marten and especially wild boar. Lynx have been seen, but doubt has been cast on sightings of the Marsican bear. The birdlife in the park's mountains is varied. Foremost is the golden eagle, which is easily spotted in the area. Some rarer species, such as the peregrine falcon and the goshawk, are also present. Alpine choughs and wall creepers are common too.

 2

SPOLETO

 E5 **Perugia** **Rome-Ancona line** **Largo Ferrer 6; www.comune.spoleto.pg.it**

Likely founded by the Umbri, this striking hilltop city came under Roman control in the 3rd century BCE, transforming into a major colony thanks partly to its proximity to the Via Flaminia. Spoleto later became the seat of a Lombard dukedom and then, in the Middle Ages, an important commune. Today, the city is known for its historic monuments, including an impressive fortress, and as the home of the world-famous Festival dei Due Mondi.

① San Nicolò

Via Cecili

What looks like a single church is, in fact, a complex of religious buildings placed one on top of the other over the course of the centuries. The Gothic church, which hosted Martin Luther in 1512, has been deconsecrated and is now used for plays and concerts.

Near Via dell' Anfiteatro lie the ruins of a 2nd-century-CE Roman amphitheatre.

② San Gregorio Maggiore

Piazza Garibaldi

Just over Ponte Sanguinario, the gateway to the city is Piazza Garibaldi, home to the church of San Gregorio Maggiore. It was founded in the 4th century, in the early Christian era, outside the walls, as were all the oldest churches in the city. The structure was renovated in the 12th century, incorporating materials from various Roman remains, and a second set of city walls were built around the church. The façade is adorned with statues and a huge campanile and has a portico modelled in the style of the duomo (p155). The Romanesque interior still bears traces of medieval frescoes.

③ San Domenico

Via Pierleone

Originally built in the 13th century, the large monastic church of San Domenico was restored to its original Gothic form in the 1930s. Outside, it has a distinctive pink-and-white striped design, while inside there's a single, unusually long nave. Here, you can admire frescoes dating from the 14th and 15th centuries. In particular, take time to admire the Cappella di San Pietro Martire (the first on the left), the Cappella di Santa Maria Maddalena, on the right-hand side of the apse, and the Cappella Benedetti di Montevecchio, on the left of the presbytery.

↑ Looking over the pretty hilltop city of Spoleto

④

Santi Giovanni e Paolo

🏛 Via Filitteria

This deconsecrated church, dedicated to saints John and Paul in 1174, is worth a visit for the frescoes inside. The oldest fresco is the one depicting the *Martyrdom of Thomas Becket*, painted after his canonization in 1173.

⑤

Palazzo Collicola Arti Visive

🏛 Piazza Collicola 1
🕐 10:30am-1pm & 3:30-7pm Wed-Mon 🌐 palazzo collicola.it

The collection in this modern art gallery is divided into themed sections. The most interesting is the "Premio Spoleto", which exhibits works by contemporary Italian artists who participated in the Spoleto Prize. The event took place in 1953–1968 to gather acquisitions for a modern art collection. Among the artists who

participated were Giulio Turcato and Pino Pascali. International artists featured include Isamu Noguchi, Beverly Pepper, Alexander Calder and Alberto Burri (*p69*).

⑥

Teatro Romano

🏛 Museo Archeologico Nazionale, Piazza della Libertà

Piazza della Libertà, the site of a restored Roman theatre built in the 1st century CE, was excavated in the late 19th century. It has a capacity of 3,000 and is used during the Festival dei Due Mondi (*p53*) to stage shows. The theatre forms part of the **Museo Archeologico Nazionale**, which also occupies the monastery of Sant'Agata, one of the oldest religious buildings in the city. The museum displays finds from the city's origins in the mid-Bronze Age to its pre-Roman period.

Museo Archeologico Nazionale
🔲 🏛 Via Sant'Agata 18
📞 0743 223 277 🕐 8:30am-1pm Thu-Sun

Must See

DRINK

DaAL Wine & Food Bar

This stylish bar offers excellent wine and cocktails. Its famous happy hours are best enjoyed on the patio.

🏛 Via G Mameli 16
📞 3318 485 221

Ganzo

A trendy garden restaurant, Ganzo serves casual fare, cocktails and craft beers.

🏛 Piazza Giuseppe Garibaldi 31 🌐 ganzo.top

Spoleto Railway Station Bar

If you need one last espresso before catching your train, duck in here. The bar also sells delicious baked goods.

🏛 Piazzale Giovanni Polvani 2
📞 0743 670 604

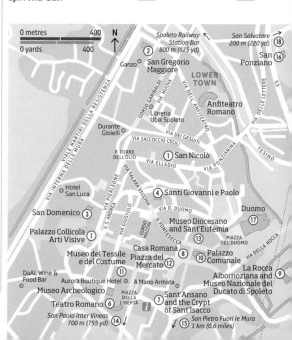

↑ Cortile d'Onore, the courtyard of honours, at La Rocca Albornoziana

SHOP

A Mano Armata

This concept store is packed with hand-crafted items, from clothing to costume jewellery.

📍 Via Arco di Druso 4
📞 0743 674 231

Libreria Ubik Spoleto

The shelves of this bookstore are packed floor-to-ceiling with books. The store also hosts readings, lectures and events.

📍 Corso Giuseppe Garibaldi 71 🌐 ubiklibri.it

Durante Gioielli

Since opening this store in 1995, owner Daniela Durante has been producing beautiful filigreed jewellery.

📍 Via Porta Fuga 14
🌐 durantegioielli.it

---

⑦

Sant'Ansano and the Crypt of Sant'Isacco

📍 Via Brignone

The church of Sant'Ansano has a complex architectural history. In the 12th century, a church dedicated to both Sant'Ansano and Sant'Isacco was built on the ruins of a 1st-century temple, which was then followed by today's 18th-century building. Highlights include Roman columns, Byzantine-style frescoes and the crypt of Sant'Isacco.

---

⑧

Casa Romana

📍 Via Visiale 📞 0743 40255 🕐 10:30am–1:30pm & 2–7pm daily

Located above the ancient forum, Casa Romana is believed to have belonged to Emperor Vespasian's mother, who was a property owner in the Nursino-Spoleto area. The patrician *domus*, dating from the 1st century CE, was discovered in 1885–86 by archaeologist Giuseppe

Sordini. Excavation revealed the remains of a mosaic floor and an inscription bearing a dedication to Caligula.

---

⑨

La Rocca Albornoziana and Museo Nazionale del Ducato di Spoleto

📍 Piazza Campello 1
🚌 Piazza Campello
📞 0743 224 952 🕐 Apr–Sep: 9:30am–10:15pm daily

In 1359, when the city was an outpost of a Church intent on reconquering Umbria, Cardinal Albornoz, papal legate for Innocent VI, ordered the construction of a military fortress (*rocca*) at the highest point of the city. It was linked to the hill behind, Monteluco, by the Ponte delle Torri, which still straddles the Valle del Tessino. The escalators here can help cover the climb.

The fortress is built on a rectangular plan around two

→ Street cafés lining the Piazza del Mercato

courtyards, the Corte d'Armi and the Cortile d'Onore. Over the centuries, La Rocca has been home to a number of notable figures, among them Lucrezia Borgia, whose caprices were perhaps responsible for the naming of the tower called "della Spiritata" (the spirited one).

Inside La Rocca today is the Museo Nazionale del Ducato di Spoleto, which traces the history of Spoleto. Highlights include the frescoes in the Camera Pinta (in one of the main towers). These scenes were painted by artists from the school of Terni in the 14th–15th centuries.

Palazzo Comunale

🏛 Piazza del Comune
📞 0743 234 350

Erected in the Middle Ages, the Palazzo Comunale, today the town hall, was rebuilt in the late 1700s. Rooms hold valuable works of art, including two frescoes by Renaissance painter Giovanni di Pietro, who was also known as "Spagna", and an impressive canvas by Baroque painter Guercino. Also of note is the Sala Caput Umbriae, decorated with portraits of illustrious Spoleto inhabitants.

Museo del Tessile e del Costume

🏛 Via delle Terme 5 📞 0743 45940 🕐 10:30am-1pm & 4:30-7pm Sat & Sun (Fri: pm only; winter: to 5:30pm)

The Museo del Tessile e del Costume is dedicated to historic textiles, and contains over 2,500 artifacts spanning the 14th to the 20th centuries. These include liturgical vestments, fans and folk textiles. Highlights include paintings by Da Vinci and Giotto that feature "*tovaglie perugine*" (Perugia cloths), embroidered fabric that was used by both the clergy and nobility.

Piazza del Mercato

With an open market, shops and bars, this square at the heart of the oldest part of Spoleto is always busy. At the far end of the piazza is the Arch of Drusus, or **Arco di Druso**. This arch marked the point where the *cardo maximus* entered the forum (now Piazza del Mercato). It was erected in 23 CE in memory of the son of Emperor Tiberius.

Other monuments include a mid-18th-century fountain built with material taken from other buildings, among them a slab commemorating Pope Urban VIII.

Arco di Druso
🏛 Piazza del Mercato

Museo Diocesano and Sant'Eufemia

🏛 Palazzo Arcivescovile, Via Saffi 13 📞 0743 222 009 🕐 Apr-Oct: 10am-1pm & 2-6pm daily; Nov-Mar: 10am-5pm Fri-Sun

This palace, inside the Palazzo Arcivescovile, began with the construction of a Roman building (still partially visible), above which it is thought that the Palazzo dei Longobardi was built when Spoleto was a duchy. In the 12th century the building became part of a monastery. It turned into the bishop's palace in the 16th–17th centuries.

Inside is a collection of art and, in the courtyard, the 12th-century church of Sant'Eufemia, known for its rare women's galleries above the nave.

> **Highlights of the Museo del Tessile e del Costume include paintings by Da Vinci and Giotto that feature "*tovaglie perugine*" (Perugia cloths).**

STAY

Hotel
San Luca

Housed within a mid-19th-century building, the historic Hotel San Luca features an interior courtyard with a stone fountain. Pick from a range of beautifully decorated rooms and suites.

🏠 Via Interna
delle Mura 21
🌐 hotelsanluca.com

€€€€

Aurora
Boutique Hotel

This full-service hotel, set within the city's Roman walls, has rooms, suites and apartments. Guests can unwind at the in-house private spa.

🏠 Via dell
'Apollinare 3
🌐 boutiquehotel
aurora.it

€€€€

---

 ⑭

San Paolo inter Vineas

🏠 Via San Paolo

The first of four important churches, which form a curve around the eastern side of the historic centre of Spoleto, lies beyond the Giardino Pubblico (public gardens) and the stadium.

San Paolo inter Vineas was built on the site of an early Christian religious building, mentioned by St Gregory the Great in the 6th century. The present Romanesque church, flanked by a cloister, dates from the 12th and 13th centuries, and was skilfully restored in the late 20th century. The most important

feature inside is the early 13th-century fresco cycle, one of the oldest in the region. It depicts the *Prophets* and *Scenes from the Creation of the World*.

---

 ⑮

San Pietro Fuori
le Mura

🏠 Via Matteotti, then Via Pio IX, beyond the Strada Statale Flaminia

San Pietro Fuori le Mura ("outside the walls") lies south of the city centre. It stands at the top of a flight of steps on a plateau, from where there are fine views.

The building has ancient origins, probably dating back to the 5th century, when the relics of the chain of St Peter were moved here. The current church dates mainly from the 12th century. The carved stone reliefs on the façade are regarded as one of the most prized examples of Umbrian Romanesque. The reliefs on the lower, older part of the structure, produced in the 12th and 13th centuries, are rich in symbolism. They relate complex episodes taken from medieval encyclopedias, and other religious stories linked to the life of Christ.

---

⑯

San Ponziano

🏠 Via del Cimitero, off Strada Statale Flaminia

This church lies northeast of the centre, alongside the Via

Flaminia, and at the foot of the Cinciano hill. It occupies the site of the tomb of the martyr Ponziano, patron saint of Spoleto, who is commemorated on 14 January. A convent church, it was first the home of Poor Clares and later Augustinian nuns. The building has a Romanesque exterior and an interior which was completely restructured in 1788 by Giuseppe Valadier. (He also designed the doors and altars of the cathedral.)

The main feature of interest in the church is the crypt. Divided into three aisles, like the church above, and with five apses, this contains Roman fragments and some truly beautiful votive frescoes, which include one showing the Archangel Michael with a globe and staff, in the right-hand apse. On the left, meanwhile, is a fresco of an Enthroned Madonna.

→

The 15th-century portico and embellished façade of the Duomo and *(inset)* its altar featuring a painted ceiling

---

> ## Did You Know?
>
> In 217 BCE, Hannibal and his army attacked Spoleto while en route to the Alps and Rome.

INSIDER TIP
Spoleto Festival

From late June to mid-July, Spoleto becomes one big stage for 17 days as it hosts the Festival dei Due Mondi *(www. festivaldispoleto.com)*. Held since 1958, the festival sees events at venues across town.

Duomo

🏛 **Piazza del Duomo**
🕐 **10:30am-6pm daily (Sun & hols: from 12:30pm; Nov-Mar: to 5pm Mon-Sat)**

Spoleto's famous cathedral is dedicated to Santa Maria Assunta. Its façade is one of the most superb examples of Umbrian Romanesque and is decorated with a 13th-century mosaic of Solsternus and five beautiful rose windows. The portico, with its magnificent central door, was added at the end of the 15th century, while the bronze bust of Urban VIII above the central door was sculpted by Gian Lorenzo Bernini in 1640.

The interior of the church, rebuilt in Baroque style in 1648, is set on a Latin cross plan, divided into three aisles separated by a colonnade. Past the entrance, on the right, is the Cappella del Vescovo Costantino Eroli, built in 1497 and entirely decorated with frescoes by Pinturicchio. The apse has a cycle of frescoes (1467–9) chronicling the life of Mary by Filippo Lippi, whose remains are in the right transept.

On the two sides of the apse are two chapels, the Cappella della Santissima Icona and the Cappella del Sacramento. In the first is an image of the Virgin in the form of an icon, much venerated because it is attributed to St Luke. On the left is the lovely Cappella delle Reliquie. This chapel contains a 14th-century wooden statue of a *Madonna and Child* and a letter written by St Francis to his disciple Fra Leone. On the left hangs a *Crucifix* by Alberto Sotio, dated 1187. Other similar treasures are kept in the Archivio Capitolare.

San Salvatore

🏛 **Via del Cimitero, off Strada Statale Flaminia**
🕐 **For renovations**

A UNESCO-protected site, the church of San Salvatore is an exceptional example in Umbria of a building constructed using mainly salvaged material. Most of the architectural features in this three-aisled basilica date from the Roman period. For this reason, it has been difficult for art historians to date San Salvatore with any great precision, although it is undoubtedly one of the oldest churches in the country. Two theories circulate currently. According to the first, the church dates from the early Christian period, and bears witness to the heights of splendour achieved in late Roman art in this area; the Tempietto del Clitunno *(p139)* would be of the same era). According to the second theory, the building was probably designed around the 8th century.

❸

TERNI

🅐 D6 🚗 75 km (47 miles) SE of Orvieto 🚆 Rome-Anconaline 🚌 ❼ Via Cassian Bon 4 (behind Piazza Tacito); www.turismo.comune.terni.it

Set at the centre of a plain, and at the confluence of the River Nera and the Serra and Tescino streams, Terni has always been the most developed centre for industry in the region. Its industrial importance made it a target for heavy bombardment during World War II and today, despite its Bronze Age origins, it looks modern compared to most other Umbrian towns and cities. It is also the unlikely birthplace of St Valentine, the patron of lovers and one of the world's most popular saints.

① Sant'Alò

🅐 Via Sant'Alò 📞 0744 546 563 🕐 By appt, call ahead

Just off Via XI Febbraio, this Romanesque church dates from the 11th century and is notable for the abundant re-use of Roman statuary on the exterior. It is thought that the church was built on the ruins of an earlier pagan temple.

② Anfiteatro Romano

🅐 Via del Vescovado 7 📞 3426 241 721 🕐 10am-1pm & 5-8pm Thu-Sun by appt, call ahead

While this 1st-century-CE amphitheatre is very much a ruin, it is still considered one of the best-preserved Roman sites in Terni. Used as a quarry and later covered

↑ Piazza della Repubblica, a short stroll from the church of San Salvatore

by buildings, it was rediscovered in the mid-19th century and was finally excavated in the 1930s. On the left is Palazzo Vescovile, whose curvilinear rear façade follows the line of the old bastions. There are lovely views from the adjacent public gardens.

③ San Salvatore

🅐 Largo San Salvatore 🕐 8:30am-5:30pm daily (to 1pm Sun)

Just off Piazza Europa is the city's most interesting church, which was erected on the ruins of Roman buildings, but it has been impossible to establish exactly when. Also known as *Tempio del Sole* (Temple of the Sun), the main body of this church was built on a circular plan and thought to have been a Roman temple to the sun.

It is now believed to date from the 11th century; the rectangular avant-corps, meanwhile, was likely built in the 12th century.

Inside the church are traces of frescoes; the ones in the Cappella Manassei date from the 14th century. In a niche at the centre of the apse is a jewelled cross, and above that is a fragmented *Madonna with Child and Saint*, and a 16th-century *Crucifixion*.

the public gardens, was built on the site of earlier religious buildings, the first of which existed at least by the 6th century; numerous churches were later built on the same site. The current basilica is the result of reconstruction in 1653, although there are still some traces of a Romanesque church.

Its façade has a huge portico with three doors in the Romanesque style. The upper part of the exterior has statues of the eight bishops of Terni, including St Valentine, by Marcello Piacentini. Look out for the bird and animal reliefs on the main door as you enter.

Inside, the well-lit interior is divided into three naves, with a Cosmatesque-style floor of decorative geometric inlay stonework. There's also the Museo Diocesano e Capitolare, displaying works of religious art.

Duomo (Santa Maria Assunta)

Piazza Duomo 8am-noon & 3:30-7pm daily

The Duomo, located south of the city centre, near

← The exterior of the Duomo (Santa Maria Assunta) featuring a large portico

EAT

Urban Beer House

The menu here offers street food, salads and desserts, plus great beer.

Piazza dell'Olmo 6
urbanbeerhouse.it

€€€

Nascostoposto

This modern venue has an Italian menu.

Via Sant'Alò 10
0744 608 309

€€€

The Street Pizza Lab

Choose from over 90 varieties of pizza by the cut, made with a naturally leavened dough.

Via XX Settembre 62/B thestreet pizzalab.it

€€€

---

⑤ 🎨 🏛

Centro Arti Opificio SIRI (CAOS)

📍Via Franco Molé 25
📞0744 1031 864 🕐10am-1pm & 5-8pm Thu-Sun

This former 5,600-sq-m (60,280-sq-ft) chemical plant houses the Aurelio de Felice Museum of Modern and Contemporary Art, a collection that includes lithographs by Chagall, Mirò, Picasso and Kandinsky. The museum's broad sweep also encompasses works representative of the medieval Umbrian school, such as by Benozzo Gozzoli (*The Marriage of St Catherine*), Spagna and Niccolò Alunno; pieces by up-and-coming local artists are displayed, too.

The vast complex also contains the fascinating Claudia Giontella Archaeological Museum, the 90-seat Sergio Secci Theatre and multifunctional cultural spaces, which host national and international travelling exhibitions, educational workshops and artist residencies. There's a library, a video room, labs and classrooms, too.

---

⑥

San Francesco

📍Piazza San Francesco
🕐7:30am-7pm daily

It is worth making a detour half-way along Corso Tacuto, to admire this 13th-century church, which was originally designed in typical Franciscan style with a single nave and transept. Major changes were made to the building in the 14th and 16th centuries, when the space was modified to accommodate the demands of the large Franciscan community. In the course of the 15th century, the lateral aisles and the bell tower were added; the charming bell tower is decorated with vibrant green and

ST VALENTINE

Many historians believe that the patron saint of love was born as Valentinus in Terni in the late 2nd century CE. He rose to become bishop of the city at a time when religious persecution was rife, and oversaw the marriages of many Christian couples. He was later killed, for proselytizing, on 14 February, 273 CE.

friezes and showcase ornamental motifs, which illustrate scenes from the life of the martyred apostle. Restoration work carried out on the building following World War II, when the structure was damaged by bombing, led to the rediscovery of these frescoes, which date back to the medieval era.

blue majolica tiles. Inside, the Cappella Paradisi contains a cycle of truly impressive 15th-century frescoes called *The Last Judgment*, painted by Italian painter Bartolomeo di Tommaso of the Giotto school, and which depict scenes of Paradise, Hell and the seven sins.

⑦
San Pietro

📍 Piazza San Pietro
🕐 8am–noon & 4–7pm daily

San Pietro is one of the most important Romanesque churches in Italy. Built in the 14th century, the church has been enlarged and restored several times. Its gabled façade features a Gothic rose window on top of the entrance and, to the left, a bell tower. The church is graced with horizontal and vertical sections that frame figurative

⑧
Mostra Permanente di Paleontologia

📍 Ex-chiesa di San Tommaso, Largo Liberotti
📞 0744 434 202 🕐 10am–1pm & 5–8pm Thu–Sun

A vital tool for anyone studying the early history of Umbria, this permanent exhibition, located in the former 14th-century church of San Tommaso, has a rich collection of items. The first floor showcases an interesting paleontological collection, while the second floor has displays of fossils that have been found in the region. Highlights of the museum include the remains of several ancient mammals from the Pleistocene (Ice Age) and a diorama of the region when it was covered by the waters of the ancient Tiberine Lake.

Did You Know?

The Mostra Permanente di Paleontologia displays around 300 fossils.

←

Gabled façade of the church of San Francesco with its Gothic rose window

PARCO FLUVIALE DEL NERA

AE6 **A**9 km (6 miles) E of Terni **B**Terni, Rome-Ancona line **C** **i**Parco Fluviale del Nera: Via Cassion Bon, 0744 389 966; Cascata delle Marmore: hours vary, check website; www.cascatadellemarmore.info

Stretching over 2,120 ha (5,240 acres), the Parco Fluviale del Nera is a protected parkland that incorporates diminutive villages, ancient abbeys and hermitages, and an impressive artificial waterfall.

Known as the "water park", this natural park extends along most of the River Nera, which begins its course in the Apennine mountains and then flows from Ferentillo to the lower reaches of Terni. Within the park is one of the most famous and much-loved sights in Italy, the Cascata delle Marmore, the highest waterfall in the country. Here, the water from the River Velino cascades down in three stages, over a total height of 165 m (541 ft), to reach the River Nera. Note that the water for the waterfall is switched on only for brief periods, which vary from month to month, so you should check ahead if you don't want to miss the spectacle.

As well as the falls, the park offers several outdoor activities, including watersports such as rafting, canoeing and kayaking. There are also opportunities for hikers, including the Ferentillo path to the church of Santo Stefano, and for rock climbers, particularly in the area around the village of Montefranco and the fortified settlement of Ferentillo. The latter is guarded by twin 14th-century citadels and is home to the church and crypt of Santo Stefano.

CONSTRUCTING A WATERFALL

In 271 BCE, the Romans linked the Velino and Nera rivers via the Cavo Curiano, the channel that feeds today's main waterfall. Since then, the Cascata delle Marmore has been integral to the river system of central Italy. Despite opposition, the channel was extended in the 15th and 16th centuries, led by architects such as Antonio da Sangallo, Giovanni Fontana and Carlo Maderno. The falls were also adapted for hydroelectric power during the 1920s.

↑ Rafting on the River Nera, a popular activity in the Parco Fluviale del Nera

→ The thundering yet tranquil Cascata delle Marmore falls

GREAT VIEW
Watch the Falls

The park has two main waterfall viewpoints, the Belvedere Inferiore and the Belvedere Superiore. At the latter, the Specola viewing tower is the ideal spot to witness the falls' rainbow phenomenon.

EXPERIENCE MORE

Cascia

🄰F5 🚗50 km (31 miles)
E of Spoleto 🚌 🛈Piazza
Garibaldi 1; 0743 71147

Cascia has been inhabited since late antiquity thanks to its strategic hilltop location. In the early Middle Ages, it was a Ghibelline city, locked in a bitter struggle with Norcia and Spoleto, cities owing allegiance to the pope. Taken by Rome in 1517, Cascia became important because of its position on the border with the Kingdom of Naples.

With the unification of Italy, Cascia lost its political relevance and fell into a long period of decline, halted in the 20th century thanks only to religious tourism, which brought large numbers of pilgrims dedicated to the memory of Santa Rita. The pilgrimage is still a significant feature of life in Cascia today, so the focus is no longer the ruined hilltop fortress, but a modern sanctuary dedicated to the saint. It was built in 1947, replacing a 16th-century church. To the left of the sanctuary is the convent of Santa Rita, where the saint lived for much of her life.

Other sites to visit in the town include the Museo Civico (split between the Palazzo Santi and the church of Sant'Antonio Abate), which has fine wooden sculptures, and the churches of San Francesco and Santa Maria. On the outskirts of the town is Roccaporena, Rita's birthplace, dominated by a hill known as the *scoglio* (cliff) of Santa Rita. The area's many castles and towers, which formed an effective system of fortification, are evidence of the historical importance of the region.

Norcia

🄰F5 🚗43 km (27 miles) E
of Spoleto 🚌 🛈Via Alberto
Novelli 1; www.comune.
norcia.pg.it

Found at the edge of the Parco Nazionale dei Monti Sibillini, on the edge of the

The towering façade of the Basilica of Santa Rita da Cascia ↓

A LAND RENOWNED FOR SAINTS

Two of the most important saints in Umbrian history (apart from St Francis) were born in this area. St Benedict, founder of the oldest monastic order in the West, was born (with his twin sister Santa Scolastica) in Norcia, in 480. Then, nearly 1,000 years later, Santa Rita (born Rita Lotti, commemorated on 22 May) was born at Roccaporena, near Cascia, in around 1380, and died in the mid-15th century.

↑ One of the many *salumerie* selling cured meats found in Norcia

plain of Santa Scolastica, Norcia was a trading town and a staging post for centuries. Today, the town is known for its local produce, in particular its black truffles and high-quality meat, sausages and salami. In fact, the word "norcino" – from Norcia – is now synonymous with superior meat products. Browsing the wonderful *salumerie* and other food shops is a highlight of any visit to the town.

Over the years, Norcia has been affected by a number of earthquakes. The most recent one, which took place in October 2016, destroyed most of the town's churches and cultural heritage. Despite the damage, Norcia, which is of great historic importance to the Italian people, retains its charm, and several buildings still stand or have since been rehabilitated.

Norcia's town walls were originally built by the Romans (who conquered the town in 290 BCE), but were replaced by another, heart-shaped set in the 13th century. As with the town, these mighty walls have been damaged by the disastrous earthquakes over the years. Despite this, the ancient gates that dot the walls (eight in all) can still be seen along the perimeter of the town. One of these gates, Porta Romana, marks the start of Corso Sertorio, which

leads to the Piazza San Benedetto, the heart of the town since the Middle Ages. At the centre of this square is a statue of St Benedict, which was erected in 1880. Overlooking the square is the 14th-century Palazzo Comunale that was partly rebuilt over the years. Its portico is original, while the soaring bell tower dates from the 18th century. Alongside the palazzo stood the church of San Benedetto. Founded in the Middle Ages, the church was sadly levelled following the 2016 earthquake. The only structures that remain are the 14th-century façade, which is dominated by a monumental doorway (1578); two statues representing St Benedict and Santa Scolastica; and, on the right side of the church, the front arch of a 16th-century portico, the Portale delle Misure.

On the other side of the piazza is the impressive Castellina, a fortress that was built for Pope Julius III in 1554. It houses the **Museo Civico Diocesano**, where the highlights include two crucifixes and a five-figured sculptural group of the *Deposition* (13th century).

Museo Civico Diocesano
🅰️🕐🅿️ ⌂ Piazza San Benedetto 📞 0743 817 030
🕐 Hours vary, call ahead

SHOP

Norcineria Laudani
Located near the arched entrance into Norcia, this delicatessen sells a host of food supplies, including cured meats, fresh cheeses and sweet treats.
🅰️ F5 ⌂ Corso Sertorio 49, Norcia 🌐 norcineria laudani.com

Birra Nursia
Founded in 2012, this shop sells Birra Nursia, beer brewed by Benedictine monks. All proceeds go towards the evangelical work of the monastery.
🅰️ F5 ⌂ Via Case Sparse 164, Norcia 🌐 birranursia.it

Cioccolateria Vetusta Nursia
Head to this elegant sweetshop for handcrafted artisan chocolate delights and other sugary specialities, such as pistachio-flavoured biscuits.
🅰️ F5 ⌂ Via della Stazione 43, Norcia 🌐 cioccolateria vetustanursia.it

EAT

Ristorante Vespasia
This Michelin-starred establishment is housed in a former 16th-century noble residence. Diners choose their tasting menu ahead of arrival.
🅰️ F5 ⌂ Via Cesare Battisti 10, Norcia 🌐 vespasianorcia.com
€€€

STAY

Colle Abramo delle Vigne Agriturismo

This pet-friendly farmstay has six self-catering apartments.

 D7 Strada di Collabramo 34, Vigne colleabramo.it

€€€

Terra Umbra

This luxury property offers a host of outdoor activities and sports.

 D7 S.P. Maratta Bassa 61, Narni terraumbra.it

€€€

Casale Valigi

Elegant rooms and a saltwater pool are on offer at this pretty spot.

 D7 Strada di Colombata 11, Narni casalevaligi.it

€€€

Narni

D7 13 km (8 miles) W of Terni Rome-Ancona line Piazza dei Priori 3; www.comune.narni.tr.it

This unspoiled hilltown, perched dramatically above a bend in the River Nera, dates back to the Umbri people, who founded *Nequinum*. This settlement was conquered by Rome in 299 BCE and was renamed *Narnia*, after the nearby river. Its importance under the Romans derived from the fact that it was the birthplace of Emperor Nerva, in 32 CE, and also a major stopping point on the Via Flaminia. This major trade route helped Narni grow until it occupied the entire rocky spur above the Nera.

Most of the sights are close to the main axis of the town, formed by Via Garibaldi and Via Mazzini. At one end is Piazza Garibaldi, home of Narni's duomo, an imposing building dedicated to San Giovenale, the town's patron saint. Founded in 1047 and reconstructed in the 12th century, the duomo's façade has a portico and a portal decorated with carvings. Inside on the right is the mausoleum of the bishops of Narni, which is dominated by a tombstone dating from 558. A short walk away is the central Piazza dei Priori, the attractive seat of civic power in Narni. Facing the square are two 14th-century palazzi, the Palazzo dei Priori, with a portico and an impressive loggia, and the Palazzo del Podestà (or Palazzo Comunale), which features a series of Roman and medieval archaeological stones and finds in its atrium.

Nearby is the now deconsecrated 12th-century church of San Domenico, which houses the Public Library, Historical Archive and the town art gallery. It has some of the best medieval frescoes in Narni. San Domenico also has works from other churches in the town. Visit the Inquisition cells in the underground areas of the church to see the graffiti made by the prisoners of the ecclesiastical court. The intriguing underground of the town can also be toured via **Narni Sotterranea**.

Another important church in Narni is the 14th-century San Francesco, built on the

Did You Know?

C S Lewis named the fictional realm depicted in *The Chronicles of Narnia* after Narni's Latin name.

site where it is said that St Francis stayed during his sojourn here in 1213, and where he founded an oratory. The church is Romanesque, but with some Gothic elements. The façade has an impressive doorway, with a niche above. Inside, frescoes adorn every inch of wall: of special interest are those by Italian painter, Mezzastris.

On top of the hill that dominates Narni is a 14th-century fortress known as the Rocca. It was built by Gattapone, at the behest of Cardinal Albornoz, who was responsible for numerous fortresses which still bear his name. Narni's fortress was abandoned for years, but it has now been restored.

Heading out of Narni, towards Terni, a short detour to the left brings you to a bridge over the River Nera. This is the best possible observation point from which to admire a majestic Roman arch in the middle of the river, the only one surviving from the Ponte d'Augusto. It was once one of the most popular sights on the Grand Tour.

Continuing along the same road, over the River Nera, a

←

Looking towards the picturesque hilltop town of Narni

climb leads to the Abbazia di San Cassiano, one of the most important religious buildings that dot the countryside surrounding Narni. Set in a panoramic position, the Romanesque, 12th-century complex is enclosed by battlemented walls and includes a pretty church with a bell tower. To the southeast, 13 km (8 miles) from Narni, is the Convento del Sacro Speco, founded in 1213 by St Francis, who often prayed in a cave nearby. The place is imbued with a mystical atmosphere.

Narni Sotterranea

🌐 narnisotterranea.it

San Pietro in Valle

🅰E6 🚗18 km (11 miles) NE of Terni 🚉Rome-Ancona line, Terni, 20 km (12 miles); FCU Perugia-Terni line 🚌 🕐Church: hours vary, call ahead, 3286 864 226 🌐sanpietro invalle.com

It is difficult to try to rank Umbrian abbeys in order of importance, but clearly no classification could omit the Benedictine abbey of San Pietro in Valle, situated in the lower part of the Valnerina, just north of the village of Ferentillo (p160).

Set against a backdrop of wooded hills, San Pietro in Valle is of significant artistic and religious interest. The abbey's roots lie deep in legend. Its foundation, as one of the frescoes in the left-hand transept of the church testifies, traditionally dates from the 5th century CE, when the Lombard duke of Spoleto, Faroaldo II, met the Syrian hermit Lazarus. St Peter had suggested to the duke in a dream that he should transform the hermit's small chapel into a powerful abbey, and so San Pietro in Valle was built. Faroaldo later decided to stay here, becoming a monk, and he rests here still: his splendid sarcophagus can be seen in the right-hand transept. The abbey was severely damaged by the Saracens in the 9th century, but was restored in around 1000 by Ottone III and then by his successor, Enrico II. In the 1930s, extensive renovation revealed the medieval linear forms which the building had managed to retain, despite all the alterations. Today, the abbey is privately owned, and has been converted into an appealing, sought-after hotel and restaurant, part of the Relais & Châteaux chain, though parts are open to the general public.

The abbey church is owned by the state and is well worth a visit. Long and formal, with a single nave ending in a short transept and three apses, the church contains some superb works of art. On the walls is a cycle of frescoes, which ranks among the finest examples of Romanesque painting in Italy. The inner façade and transept are decorated with works from later eras.

Look out for the beautifully preserved Lombard altar (8th century), which bears the self-portrait and signature of the sculptor: "Ursus".

↑ Horses grazing in front of the abbey of San Pietro in Valle

A 12th-century fresco in the Benedictine abbey of San Pietro in Valle

⑨
Carsulae

🅰 D6 🚗 15 km (9 miles) NW of Terni 🚆 Rome-Ancona line, Terni, 14 km (9 miles); FCU Perugia-Terni line 🚌 ℹ️ Sito Archeologico di Carsulae; 8:30am–1pm & 2–6:30pm Tue–Sun; www.carsulae.site

This ruined Roman town was founded in the 3rd century BCE on the slopes of the mound bearing the name of Chiccirichì.

At first merely a staging and garrison post, then a village, Carsulae eventually became a town in Augustus' Region VI. It experienced its greatest period of splendour between 30 and 10 BCE, when work was being done on the Via Flaminia. The town was abandoned following the decline in importance of the road and because it was raided by marauders on a number of occasions.

From the 16th century onwards, the aristocratic families of the region, in particular the Cesi family of Acquasparta, began to carry out excavations in search of objects of interest for their own private collections. The modern archaeological excavations date back to the 1950s, when a number of sites were uncovered, including a basilica, the old forum and temples. The great value of Carsulae as an archaeological site lies in the fact that the original layout has mostly remained complete despite the encroachment of the modern Via Flaminia, which crosses the site.

The 11th-century church of San Damiano was built using the remains of a Roman temple. Nearby is the forum, with an adjacent basilica featuring three aisles and an apse. In front of the forum is a public square where numerous low walls – the ruins of religious and secular buildings – can be seen: among them are the bases of the Tempietti Gemelli (twin temples) and the remains of baths.

The town is also home to the Arco di San Damiano, a monumental gate which once had three arches: only the central one survives. A burial site is also nearby. Beyond the modern Via Flaminia is the Amphitheatre, used for circus games, and the theatre; sadly only the foundations of the stage and the supports for the stalls (orchestra seats) remain.

↑ Remains of the Arco di San Damiano in the ancient town of Carsulae

⑩
Acquasparta

🅰 D6 🚗 22 km (13 miles) NW of Terni 🚆 Rome-Ancona line, Terni, 20 km (12 miles); FCU Perugia-Terni line 🚌 ℹ️ Piazza del Mercato 1; 3336 162 099

The first records of Acquasparta date from the 10th century. The name derives from the local spa waters, which were known to the Romans and, it is said, taken by St Francis. Acquasparta's appearance today recalls the influence of the Cesi family, who changed the face of the town during the 15th and 16th centuries. Among the features dating from this era are a palace named after the noble family, and the walls and towers.

Palazzo Cesi, commissioned by the Cesi family from the

> Acquasparta's name derives from the local spa waters, which were known to the Romans and, it is said, taken by St Francis.

architect Giovanni Domenico Bianchi, was completed in 1565. The interior of this aristocratic residence is richly decorated, featuring rooms with splendid coffered wooden ceilings. The one in the Sala di Ercole (Room of Hercules) is particularly fine. The palazzo belongs to the University of Perugia and is used for seminars and conferences, and also hosts a summer art exhibition.

Along the main street, Corso Umberto I, are the church of Santa Cecilia and the Oratorio del Sacramento, where a mosaic floor from the ruins of Roman Carsulae can be seen.

⑪ San Gemini

D6 🚗 13 km (8 miles) NW of Terni 🚉 Rome-Ancona line, Terni, 11 km (7 miles); FCU Perugia-Terni line 🚌 🛈 Piazza San Francesco 4; 0744 630130

The medieval town of San Gemini was built over the ruins of an ancient Roman settlement, alongside the Via Flaminia. The only traces of the Roman town are a tomb, the so-called Grotta degli Zingari and a ruined villa.

At the heart of San Gemini is Piazza di Palazzo Vecchio, home to the medieval Palazzo Pubblico, whose tower was much altered in the 1700s. Under an exterior arcade is an image of St George, patron saint of the town. The 13th-century Oratorio di San Carlo, nearby, has lovely frescoes.

Outside the town walls are the churches of San Francesco, with a fine Gothic doorway, and San Giovanni Battista, featuring a lovely façade with a richly decorated Romanesque door. One of the façade inscriptions bears the date of its founding, 1199, with the names of the architects and sculptors, Nicola, Simone and Bernardo.

Just outside San Gemini's old gateway is the privately owned church of San Nicolò. Its Romanesque portal is a copy, since the original is in the Metropolitan Museum in New York. There's also an interactive science museum, Geolab, for children and those interested in geology.

To the north, on flatter ground, lies the modern spa town of San Gemini Fonte, offering facilities for spa water treatments.

TOP 3 WINERIES IN SOUTHERN UMBRIA

Leonardo Bussoletti
🛆 D6 🏠 Località Pianello 175 A, San Gemini 🌐 leonardobussoletti.it
This vineyard makes delicious wines with care; visit the cellar in San Gemini for a tasting.

Cantine Zanchi
🛆 C6 🏠 SP8 Amelia-Orte Km 4, Amelia 🌐 cantinezanchi.it
High-quality, organic wines are crafted at this third-generation cellar.

Tenuto Pizzogallo
🛆 C6 🏠 SP8 Amelia-Orte Km 5, Amelia 🌐 pizzogallo.it
With an enchanting estate, this agriturismo is studded with vineyards and olive groves.

Piazza San Francesco, one of San Gemini's pretty squares ↑

Panorama of the ancient town of Amelia perched on a hill ↑

⑫

Amelia

🅐C6 🏠26 km (16 miles) W of Terni 🚉 Narni, 11 km (7 miles), Rome-Ancona line 🚌 ℹ Piazza Augusto Vera 10; www.turismo amelia.it

Balancing on a hill between the Tiber and Nera valleys, Amelia is another Umbrian town of ancient origin. In fact, it was in antiquity that the town knew its greatest importance, when it was located on the Via Amerina, one of several Roman roads linking southern Etruria with Umbria.

Still standing today are parts of the impressive Mura Poligonali (Polygonal Walls), built by the Umbri and among the oldest of their kind in Italy. Believed to date from the 5th century BCE, the walls are 8 m (26 ft) high, and 3 m (10 ft) wide. The bastions are mostly made up of vast polygonal stone blocks, fitted together without mortar. The size of the walls can be best appreciated at Porta Romana, framed by a Classical-style 17th-century arch. This same gate is also the main entrance to the historic centre. Close by, in Palazzo Boccarini, is the

Museo Archeologico, home to all manner of Roman finds from tablets to sarcophagi.

A short way up Via della Repubblica is the 13th-century church of Santi Filippo e Giacomo, which has seven tombs of the Geraldini family, one of the most important dynasties in Amelia. Cardinal Alessandro Geraldini is famous for persuading the Spanish monarchy to authorize Christopher Columbus's first voyage to the Indies. The church's funerary monuments include the 15th-century tombs of Elisabetta and Matteo Geraldini, the work of Agostino di Duccio.

Palazzo Farrattini, just off Via della Repubblica, is the most impressive private building. It was designed in the 16th century for the Farrattini. Via della Repubblica climbs further to Piazza Marconi, the town's lovely main square, and then continues up Via Duomo to the highest point of the city and the duomo.

The cathedral's appearance today is the result of its reconstruction in the 17th century, which replaced the original Romanesque church, though the fine bell tower remains. Inside are several key works of art including a panel with a *Madonna and*

CISTERNS

Built by the Romans, cisterns were large underground reservoirs for storing water. These are still visible today in some towns, along with their wells. Amelia's reservoirs are particularly impressive; they are made up of ten parallel tanks with a capacity of storing around 4.5 million litres (1 million gallons) of water.

Child attributed to Antoniazzo Romano, and two paintings by Niccolò Pomarancio in the Oratorio del Sacramento.

The area around Amelia is dotted with abbeys and sanctuaries that are easy to reach. About 4 km (2 miles) southwest of Amelia, on the road to Attigliano, is the 13th-century Monastery of the Santissima Annunziata, which belongs to the Friars Minor. Heading eastwards, past the village of Capitone, you reach the village of La Cerqua and the Sanctuary of the Madonna della Quercia. This was built in the 16th century to hold an image of the Virgin Mary, now on the apse altar.

Museo Archeologico

 🗺 Piazza Augusto Vera 10 🕐 Hours vary, check website 🌐 ameliamusei.it

---

13
Lugnano in Teverina

🗺 C6 🗺 35 km (22 miles) W of Terni 🚆 Attigliano, 11km (7 miles), Milan-Rome line 🚌 𝒊 Pro Loco, Piazza S Maria 1; 0744 902566

Set in a panoramic position along a ridge and enclosed by medieval walls, this small town began life as the feudal village of a Provençal count, in around 1000 CE.

Although some way from the usual tourist trails, Lugnano is well worth visiting simply to see one of the most interesting Romanesque churches in all of Umbria, the church of Santa Maria Assunta. The building dates from the 12th century, although it has undergone extensive restoration, especially in the 15th century. In common with various other Umbrian churches of the same era, such as the cathedral of Spoleto, the façade features a beautifully decorated portico, some of which is the work of the famous Roman marble workers, the Cosmati. There is more Cosmati work inside, both in the nave (which has a striking Cosmatesque pavement) and in the crypt, which also has a finely sculpted screen. Other works of art found here include a triptych of the *Annunciation* by Niccolò Alunno, in the apse, and a *Crucifixion* of the Giotto school.

Heading 5 km (3 miles) north out of town, the S205 leads to the medieval town of Alviano, birthplace of condottiere Bartolomeo di Alviano. From here, steps lead to Santa Illuminata, a pilgrimage site linked to an order of hermits called the Camaldolese.

A lovely 10-km (6-mile) stretch of the Via Amerina runs to Montecchio, with an interesting necropolis (6th–4th centuries BCE) nearby.

14
Santa Pudenziana

🗺 D7 🗺 Strada di Visciano, Visciano 🚆 Narni-Amelia 🕐 Apr-Oct: 4-7pm Sun 🌐 santapudenziana.org

Heading south from Narni, a tortuous but scenic road leads up to the hilltop hamlet of Visciano. The reason for coming here is to visit the small and simple church of Santa Pudenziana. This is a typical example of Umbrian Romanesque, built in the 12th and 13th centuries, and making abundant use of Roman materials from the area. It has a tall stone campanile and a sober façade with a small portico. The interior is divided into three aisles, with an inlaid floor of precious marble and fragments of Roman mosaics.

The church is famous for its frescoes. Behind the façade are *Christ, San Vittore* and *San Medico*, and other saints, as well as the *Madonna and Child*, all contemporary with the construction. The other figures, such as *Santa Pudenziana*, date from the 14th and 15th centuries.

Did You Know?

St Pudenziana was martyred for refusing to worship Roman emperors as gods.

NEED TO KNOW

Cycling around Castelluccio di Norcia

BEFORE
YOU GO

Things change, so plan ahead to make the most of your trip. Be prepared for all eventualities by considering the following points before you travel.

AT A GLANCE

CURRENCY
Euro (EUR)

AVERAGE DAILY SPEND

SAVE	SPEND	SPLURGE
€50	€100	€200+

BOTTLED WATER	COFFEE	BEER	DINNER FOR TWO
€2.00	€1.00	€5.00	€60

ESSENTIAL PHRASES

Hello	Buongiorno
Goodbye	Arrivederci
Please	Per favore
Thank you	Grazie
You're welcome	Prego
Do you speak English?	Parla inglese?

ELECTRICITY SUPPLY
Power sockets are type F and L, fitting two and three-pronged plugs. Standard voltage is 220-230v.

Passports and Visas

For entry requirements, including visas, consult your nearest Italian embassy or check the **Polizia di Stato** website. Citizens of the UK, US, Canada, Australia and New Zealand do not need a visa for stays of up to three months but in future must apply in advance for the European Travel Information and Authorization System (**ETIAS**); roll-out has continually been postponed so check the website for details. Visitors from other countries may also require an ETIAS, so check before travelling.
ETIAS
W travel-europe.europa.eu/etias_en
Polizia di Stato
W poliziadistato.it

Government Advice

It is important to consult both your and the Italian government's advice before travelling. The **UK Foreign, Commonwealth and Development Office**, the **US State Department**, the **Australian Department of Foreign Affairs and Trade** and the Italian Polizia di Stato offer the latest information on security, health and local regulations.
Australian Department of Foreign Affairs and Trade
W smartraveller.gov.au
UK Foreign, Commonwealth and Development Office
W gov.uk/foreign-travel-advice
US State Department
W travel.state.gov

Customs Information

You can find information on the laws relating to goods and currency taken in or out of Italy on the Your Europe website.
Your Europe
W europa.eu

Insurance

We recommend taking out a comprehensive insurance policy covering medical care, theft, loss of belongings, cancellations and delays, and reading the small print carefully.

EU and UK citizens are eligible for free emergency medical care provided they have a valid European Health Insurance Card (EHIC) or Global Health Insurance Card (**GHIC**). Australia has a reciprocal healthcare agreement with Italy; citizens can access essential medical treatment if they are registered to **Medicare**. Visitors from elsewhere must arrange private medical insurance.

GHIC
🆆 ghic.org.uk
Medicare
🆆 humanservices.gov.au/individuals/medicare

Vaccinations

No inoculations are needed for Italy.

Booking Accommodation

Italy offers a huge variety of accommodation, from simple *pensione* (basic rooms) to luxury hotels and resorts. To avoid disappointment and inflated prices, book well in advance.

In most cities you will be charged an obligatory city tax on top of the price for the room (usually a few euros per person per night), with payment potentially requested in cash. Under Italian law, hotels need to register guests with the local police and issue a receipt of payment (*ricevuta fiscale*), which you must keep until you leave Italy.

Money

Most establishments accept major credit, debit and pre-paid currency cards. Contactless payments are becoming increasingly common in Italy, but it's always a good idea to carry some cash for smaller items such as coffee, gelato and pizza-by-the-slice, and when visiting markets or more remote areas. Cash may also be needed for public transport ticket machines. Wait staff should be tipped €1–2 and hotel porters and housekeeping will expect €1 per bag or day.

Travellers with Specific Requirements

Umbria's historic towns can be tricky to navigate for travellers with specific requirements. However, some museums and state-run attractions have facilities, with the Galleria Nazionale dell'Umbria (*p86*) offering elevators for those with limited mobility. Always call a location ahead to ensure that your needs will be met.

The **Sage Traveling** website provides lots of up-to-date information for travellers with disabilities in Italy. Trenitalia (*p177*) can also arrange special reservations and assistance at stations.

Sage Travelling
🆆 sagetraveling.com

Language

The official language is Italian. Most restaurants, hotels and attractions have at least some English-speaking staff, but local residents will appreciate efforts to speak Italian, even if only a few words.

Opening Hours

Situations can change quickly and unexpectedly. Always check before visiting attractions and hospitality venues for up-to-date opening hours and booking requirements.

Lunchtime Many stores and businesses close 1–4pm for a lunchtime *pausa* (pause).
Monday Many museums are closed.
Sunday Some stores close all day.

PUBLIC HOLIDAYS	
1 Jan	New Year's Day
6 Jan	Epiphany
Mar/Apr	Easter Sunday
Mar/Apr	Easter Monday
25 Apr	Liberation Day
1 May	Labour Day
2 Jun	Republic Day
15 Aug	Ferragosto
1 Nov	All Saints' Day
8 Dec	Feast of the Immaculate Conception
25 Dec	Christmas Day
26 Dec	St Stephen's Day

GETTING AROUND

Whether you're visiting Umbria for a weekend, a week or longer, discover how best to reach your destination and travel like a pro.

AT A GLANCE

PUBLIC TRANSPORT COSTS

PERUGIA

€1.50

70 mins
on Minimetrò

ORVIETO

€1.30

90 mins
on funicular

ASSISI

€1.30

90 mins
on bus

TOP TIP
For discounted travel on buses, trains and more, buy an Umbria.Go ticket (p178).

SPEED LIMIT

MOTORWAY	DUAL CARRIAGEWAYS
130 km/h (80mp/h)	**110** km/h (65mp/h)

SINGLE CARRIAGEWAYS	URBAN AREAS
90 km/h (55mp/h)	**50** km/h (30mp/h)

Arriving by Air

Budget carriers fly into Perugia's **San Francesco d'Assisi**, Umbria's only airport, from a number of domestic and European locations. The airport is easily accessed from Perugia and Assisi by taxi or by taking the **Umbria Airlink** bus.

To reach the region, it's also possible to fly into Rome's Ciampino, Florence's Amerigo Vespucci and Pisa's Galileo Galilei airports, all of which host national and European flights. For international flights, Rome's Leonardo da Vinci (Fiumicino) airport is the most convenient for reaching Umbria. There are excellent train links between these larger cities and those in Umbria.

San Francesco d'Assisi
W airport.umbria.it/en/home-en

Umbria Airlink
W fsbusitalia.it/content/fsbusitalia/it/turismo/servizi-speciali/umbria-airlink.html

Train Travel

International Train Travel
Regular high-speed international trains connect Italy's major rail stations to the main towns and cities in Austria, Germany, France, Switzerland and Eastern Europe. Note, however, that there are no direct trains from Umbria to European destinations; all require at least one transfer in a larger Italian city.

Reservations for these services are essential and tickets are booked up quickly. Book tickets via **Eurail** and **Interrail**.

Eurail
W eurail.com

Interrail
W interrail.eu

Domestic Train Travel
Regular train services connect most of Umbria's major cities with ease, including Assisi, Perugia and Spoleto, as well as several of the lakeside towns around Lago Trasimeno. Outside of the region, there are a number of direct services south to Rome's Termini train station, while services to northern Italy usually involve a transfer in Florence or Bologna.

GETTING TO AND FROM SAN FRANCESCO D'ASSISI AIRPORT

Transport	Journey time	Fare
Airlink bus to Perugia centre	30 mins	€5
Airlink bus to Assisi centre	35 mins	€5
Taxi to Perugia or Assisi centre	20 mins	€20-25

All services, whether slower regional or high-speed intercity trains, are run by **Trenitalia**, Italy's national rail service. Safety and hygiene measures, timetables, ticket information, transport maps and more can be obtained from the Trenitalia website.

Train tickets can be purchased in stations, at certain tobacco shops or online via the Trenitalia website. Tickets for regional trains must be validated prior to boarding, whether through an email for e-tickets or at the green ticket machines found inside stations for paper tickets. All other tickets do not require validation. It's a good idea to book all trains in advance.

Note that many train stations in Umbria are located outside of a city's historic centre, and often not within walking distance. Most have public buses that run between the two; however, buses might not run at night.

Trenitalia
W trenitalia.com/en.htmlPublic Transport

Public Transport

Umbria's public transport largely revolves around buses, although Lago Trasimeno has a ferry service, Perugia has a Minimetrò and Orvieto has a funicular. Bus and ferry services are run by **Busitalia** (part of Trenitalia), whose website provides information on timetables, tickets and more.

Busitalia
W fsbusitalia.it

Buses

Most cities and towns in Umbria are served by buses, which also travel between different settlements in the area, and are a great way of getting to places not covered by trains.

Busitalia tickets can be purchased either at vending machines found in bus stations or via newspaper kiosks, tobacconists and bars. It's also possible to pick up a ticket once you've boarded a bus, but prices are higher. Another option is to download SALGO, Busitalia's app, which allows you to purchase tickets, plan your journey and find your stop; see the Busitalia website for further details.

Ferries

Umbria's ferry service is centred on Lago Trasimeno. Boats run between a number of settlements around the lake, such as Passignano sul Trasimeno and Castiglione del Lago, as well as to the islands within it. Services usually run several times a day, depending on the specific route in question, with greater frequency at weekends and during the summer months.

Depending on the trip being made, single tickets can range from €4.20 to €5.40, while round-trip tickets range from €6 to €10. If you're planning to visit multiple destinations on the lake, you can also purchase a full-day ticket for €14.30. A daily supplement of €2.20 is charged for bikes and medium to large dogs. Tickets can be bought from pier-side offices at the main towns around the lake.

Minimetrò

The single-line Minimetrò in Perugia runs from the Porta Nova car park (Pian di Massiano stop) on the city's edge into the historic centre (Pincetto stop).

Tickets can be purchased by cash or card from automatic dispensers, which are usually located at the entrance of each station. It's also possible to buy them from participating tobacconists, cafés and newsstands. The tickets, known as Unico Perugia (UP), are valid on buses as well as the Minimetrò. Single tickets, covering 70 minutes of travel, cost €1.50. Other ticket options include a 24-hour Tourist Ticket (€5.40) or a multitrip ticket covering ten 70-minute journeys (€12.90).

Minimetrò
W minimetrospa.it

Funicular

Orvieto's funicular whisks visitors from the city's train station, found on the outskirts of town, to Piazza Cahen on the edge of the historic centre. Running daily, it's a cost-effective and scenic way to reach the centre, costing just €1.30 for a single ticket and offering views over the surrounding countryside. For more information, visit the Orvieto Viva website (p180).

Tickets

For visitors planning to use a variety of transport within the region, Busitalia's Umbria.GO ticket is a worthwhile purchase. It covers travel on buses, regional trains and Lago Trasimeno ferries, as well as Perugia's Minimetrò and Orvieto's funicular. You can purchase tickets for 1 day (€15), 3 days (€33) or 7 days (€45). If you're visiting the area for a longer period, it can be worth purchasing an Umbria.GO 30 subscription (€120), which is valid for one calendar month. Pick up tickets from any Busitalia or Trenitalia ticket office.

Taxis

Taxis are not hailed; find one at an official taxi stand (usually located at train stations or main piazzas), or reserve one by phone. Note that taxis may not be readily available at night, especially at smaller train stations. Taxi apps such as Uber and Lyft do not operate in Umbria.

Driving

Thanks to a network of well-maintained and signposted roads, driving in Umbria is easy and convenient, and is often the best way to reach small towns not served by rail or bus.

Driving to Umbria

Drivers coming from Milan and Florence, in Italy's north, can take the A1, which runs along Umbria's western edge. This motorway joins with more minor roads at Orvieto, allowing onward access to Todi and from here to the rest of the region. There's also the option to travel south via Bologna on the E45. This motorway runs through the region's centre, passing through Perugia and Terni, and providing access via more minor roads to the likes of Spoleto and Assisi. If travelling from Rome in the south, the quickest route is along the A1, exiting at Orte to join the E45, which leads to Terni. Note that the A1 is an *autostrade* and so is subject to tolls; payment is made at the end of the journey in cash or by credit card.

If you bring your own foreign-registered car into the country, you must carry a Green Card, the vehicle's registration documents, proof of car insurance and a valid driver's licence. All non-EU-registered vehicles must also display a nationality sticker at the rear.

Driving in Umbria

Most roads in Umbria are single carriageways marked SS (strada statale) or SP (strada provinciale). While generally in good condition, they're often narrow. Reaching more remote destinations, such as rural agriturismos, may require driving on hard-packed dirt roads, which may be uneven.

Many cities and towns have pedestrian-only areas where driving is forbidden or limited only to local residents and deliveries. Some places, such as Perugia, Orvieto and Terni, also enforce a Limited Traffic Zone (ZTL), which prevents access to city centres at specific times.

The potential for travelling in Umbria using an electric vehicle (EV) is growing. However, while charging points are increasingly available in urban centres, they can be sporadic in remote areas; check in advance to plan your journey using the **Open Charge Map** website.

Open Charge Map

🆆 openchargemap.org

Car Hire

To hire a car in Italy you must be over 21 and have held a valid driver's licence for at least a year. Driving licences issued by any of the EU member states are valid throughout the European Union, including Italy. If visiting from outside the EU, you may need to apply for an International Driving Permit (IDP). Check with your local automobile association.

Perugia's San Francesco d'Assisi airport (p176) has outlets of international car hire companies; they can also often be found within walking distance of train stations in larger cities.

Rules of the Road

Drive on the right, use the left lane only for passing and yield to traffic from the right. Seatbelts are required for all passengers in the front and back, and heavy fines are levied for using a mobile phone while driving. A strict drink-drive limit (p180) is enforced.

During the day, dipped headlights are compulsory when you are driving on motorways, dual carriageways and all out-of-town roads. A red warning triangle, spare tyre and fluorescent vests must be carried at all times, for use in an emergency.

In the event of an accident or breakdown, switch on your hazard warning lights and place a warning triangle 50 m (55 yd) behind your vehicle. For breakdowns call the ACI emergency number (803 116 from an Italian phone or 800 116 800 from a foreign mobile) or the emergency services (112 or 113). The ACI will tow any foreign-registered vehicle to the nearest ACI-affiliated garage for free. For hire cars, call the emergency services or the assistance number provided by the hire company.

Plotting the main driving routes according to journey time, this map is a handy reference for travelling between Umbria's main towns and cities by car. The times given reflect the fastest and most direct routes available. Tolls may apply.

··· Direct driving routes

Citta di Castello

Perugia — Assisi

Orvieto — Spoleto

Terni

Città di Castello to Perugia	45 mins
Perugia to Assisi	20 mins
Perugia to Orvieto	1.5 hrs
Orvieto to Terni	1 hr
Terni to Perugia	1.5 hrs
Terni to Spoleto	20 mins

Parking

While parking in Umbria's historic centres can be limited, large car parks are often located outside of city centres, with public transport to take you onwards. You'll usually pay upon exiting, although some public car parks require advance payment.

Cycling

Cycling in Umbria can be a joy, whether you're pootling around Lago Trasimeno (p76) or mountain biking in parks like Monte Sibillini. Some cities, such as Perugia and Terni, are good for cycling, although you'll need to be aware of pedestrianized areas. There are also several great bicycle-touring routes, including the Assisi-Spoleto Bike Lane (p142) and the Via Francigena, large sections of which are closed to traffic. The Umbria Tourism website (p180) has useful information on cycling.

Bicycle Hire

Both Perugia and Terni have bike-hire schemes run by **BicinCittà**. In Perugia you can purchase 24-hour access for €5 or 48-hour access for €9, while in Terni, 24-hour access costs €6. All cover 4 hours of bike use per day. It's possible to purchase access via the BicinCittà website or the **Weelo** app.

Most other cities and towns have outfitters that hire standard and electric bicycles for half-to multiday periods; the Umbria Tourism website (p180) provides a list of options.

BicinCittà
W bicincitta.com
Weelo
W weelo.it

Bike Safety

Cyclists in Umbria often share narrow roads with cars and other vehicles. Helmets are strongly encouraged and prudence is a necessity, especially on heavily trafficked roads. Bikes are not allowed on motorways or on some dual carriageways.

Walking

Umbria is wonderfully walkable. Once reached, hilltowns are surprisingly flat and compact, and many streets are either pedestrianized or made up of narrow lanes inaccessible to cars.

Beyond urban areas, Umbria is crisscrossed with several long-distance walking routes, such as the undulating Franciscan Path of Peace (p94). Plenty of hiking routes can be found in Umbria's national and regional parks, too, whether it's rocky summit tracks in the Parco Regionale del Monte Subasio or waterfall-dotted paths in the Parco Fluviale del Nera. The Umbria Tourism website (p180) has further information on walking routes.

PRACTICAL
INFORMATION

A little local know-how goes a long way in Umbria. Here you can find all the essential advice and information you will need during your stay.

AT A GLANCE

EMERGENCY NUMBERS

GENERAL EMERGENCY	AMBULANCE
112	**118**

FIRE SERVICE	POLICE
115	**113**

TIME ZONE

CET/CEST: Central European Summer Time runs from the last Sunday in March to the last Sunday in October.

TAP WATER

Unless otherwise stated, tap water in Umbria is safe to drink.

WEBSITES

Umbria Tourism
Umbria's official tourism website (www.umbriatourism.it/en).

Città di Perugia
The official website of the region's capital (www.turismo.comune.perugia.it).

Visit Assisi
This website has useful information for visitors to Assisi (www.visit-assisi.it/en).

Orvieto Viva
The official tourism website for Orvieto (www.orvietoviva.com/en/).

Personal Security

Umbria is a safe place to visit, but you should still take precautions to avoid incidents. Keep your bags closed and close to your body at all times, especially when in crowded tourist areas. If you have anything stolen, report the crime within 24 hours to the nearest police station and take ID with you. If you need to make an insurance claim, get a copy of the crime report (denuncia). Contact your embassy if you have your passport stolen, or in the event of a serious crime or accident.

As a rule, Italians are very accepting of all people, regardless of their race, gender or sexuality. Homosexuality was legalized in 1887 and in 1982, Italy became the third country to recognize the right to legally change your gender.

Women may receive unwanted and unwelcome attention, particularly in the form of unsolicited compliments or jeers, especially around tourist areas. If you feel threatened, head straight for the nearest police station.

Health

Italy has a world-class healthcare system. Emergency medical care in Italy is free for all EU and UK citizens providing they have an EHIC or GHIC (be sure to present this as soon as possible) and for Australian citizens with Medicare (p175). Note that you may have to pay after treatment and reclaim the money later. For visitors from other countries, payment of medical expenses is the patient's responsibility. As such, it is important to arrange comprehensive medical insurance.

Seek medicinal supplies and advice for minor ailments from pharmacies (farmacia). You can find details of the nearest 24-hour service on all pharmacy doors.

Smoking, Alcohol and Drugs

Smoking, including vaping, is banned in enclosed public places, though permitted outdoors. The possession of illegal drugs is prohibited and could result in a prison sentence.

Italy has a strict limit of 0.05 per cent BAC (blood alcohol content) for drivers. This means

that you cannot drink more than a small beer or a small glass of wine if you plan to drive. For drivers with less than three years' driving experience, and those under 21, the limit is 0.

ID

By law you must carry identification at all times in Italy. A photocopy of your passport photo page (and visa if applicable) should suffice. If you are stopped by the police you may be asked to present the original document within 12 hours.

Local Customs

Italians are relatively relaxed when it comes to etiquette. Strangers usually shake hands, while friends and family greet each other with a kiss on each cheek. However, there are some things to bear in mind. You can be fined for littering, including dropping cigarette butts, or for buying from illegal vendors, who usually sell wares such as tourist trinkets on the streets. It is also an offence to bathe in public fountains.

Visiting Churches and Cathedrals

Entrance to churches is usually free, but you may be charged a small fee to see a certain area, such as a chapel, cloister or underground ruins. Visiting may be prohibited during Mass. Dress codes usually apply but are not always strictly enforced: cover your torso and upper arms, and ensure shorts and skirts cover your knees. Shoes must be worn. In some places of worship, photography is banned.

Responsible Travel

As with elsewhere in Italy, the climate crisis is having an impact on Umbria, with an increase in hot, drought-filled summers and a decrease in the amount of rainfall and snowfall, leading to compromised harvests of grapes, olives and other produce. Do your bit to conserve water by spending less time in the shower and reusing towels if staying in hotel accommodation. Note that fountains, whether for drinking water or decoration, may be turned off during times of drought.

The region is also at risk of wildfires, so be careful when disposing of cigarette butts and

glass bottles; starting a fire, even if accidental, is deemed a criminal offence. For other eco-friendly travel tips see page 41.

Mobile Phones and Wi-Fi

EU visitors to Italy can use their devices without being affected by roaming charges. Users will be charged the same rates for data, SMS and voice calls as they would pay at home. Travellers from outside of the EU should always check with their provider.

Wi-Fi is widely available in Umbria, though signals may be weak to nonexistent when you're within the stone walls that surround many villages. Cafés and restaurants will usually give you the password for their Wi-Fi on the condition that you make a purchase.

Post

Stamps (*francobolli*) are sold in kiosks and tobacconists (*tabacchi*). Letters and postcards may take between four days and two weeks to arrive, depending on the destination.

Taxes and Refunds

VAT (called IVA in Italy) is usually 22 per cent, with a reduced rate of 4 to 10 per cent on some items. Non-EU citizens can claim an IVA rebate subject to certain conditions. It is easier to claim before you buy (you will need to show your passport to the shop assistant and complete a form). If claiming retrospectively, at the airport, present a customs officer with your purchases and a *fattura* (receipt), with your name and the amount of IVA on the item purchased. Receipts will be stamped and sent back to the vendor to issue a refund.

Discount Cards

Many cities in Umbria offer a visitor's pass or discount card, such as the Assisi Welcome Card, Spoleto Card and Orvieto Carta Unica. These provide discounts on exhibitions, events and museum entry, with some even covering the cost of public transport for the duration of your stay. Cards may be free and offer smaller discounts, or cost from €20 to €25 and offer free or discounted entry to attractions.

INDEX

Page numbers in **bold** refer to main entries.

PHRASE BOOK

IN AN EMERGENCY

Help!	Aiuto!	eye-yoo-toh
Stop!	Ferma!	fair-mah
Call a doctor.	Chiama un medico.	kee-ah-mah oon meh-dee-koh
Call an ambulance.	Chiama un' ambulanza	kee-ah-mah oon am-boo-lan-tsa
Call the police.	Chiama la polizia.	kee-ah-mah la pol-ee-tsee-ah
Call the fire brigade.	Chiama i pompieri.	kee-ah-mah ee pom-pee-air-ee
Where is the telephone?	Dov'è il telefono?	dov-eh eel teh-leh-foh-noh?
The nearest hospital?	L'ospedale più vicino?	loss-peh-dah-leh pee-oovee-chee-noh?

COMMUNICATION ESSENTIALS

Yes/No	Sì/No	see/noh
Please	Per favore	pair fah-vor-eh
Thank you	Grazie	grah-tsee-eh
Excuse me	Mi scusi	mee skoo-zee
Hello	Buon giorno	bwon jor-noh
Goodbye	Arrivederci	ah-ree-veh-dair-chee
Good evening	Buona sera	bwon-ah sair-ah
morning	la mattina	lah mah-tee-nah
afternoon	il pomeriggio	eel poh-meh-ree-joh
evening	la sera	lah sair-ah
yesterday	ieri	ee-air-ee
today	oggi	oh-jee
tomorrow	domani	doh-mah-nee
here	qui	kwee
there	la	lah
What?	Quale?	kwah-leh?
When?	Quando?	kwan-doh?
Why?	Perchè?	pair-keh?
Where?	Dove?	doh-veh

USEFUL PHRASES

How are you?	Come sta?	koh-meh stah?
Very well, thank you.	Molto bene, grazie.	moll-toh beh-neh grah-tsee-eh
Pleased to meet you.	Piacere di conoscerla.	pee-ah-chair-eh dee coh-noh-shair-lah
See you soon.	A più tardi.	ah pee-oo tar-dee
That's fine.	Va bene.	va beh-neh
Where is/are ...?	Dov'è/Dove sono ...?	dov-eh/doveh soh-noh?
How long does it take to get to ...?	Quanto tempo ci vuole per andare a ...?	kwan-toh tem-poh chee voo-oh-leh pair an-dar-eh ah...?
How do I get to ...?	Come faccio per arrivare a ...?	koh-meh fah-choh pair arri-var-eh ah...?
Do you speak English?	Parla inglese?	par-lah een-gleh-zeh?
I don't understand.	Non capisco.	non ka-pee-skoh
Could you speak more slowly, please?	Può parlare più lentamente, per favore?	pwoh par-lah-reh pee-oo len-ta-men-teh pair fah-vor-eh
I'm sorry.	Mi dispiace.	mee dee-spee-ah-cheh

USEFUL WORDS

big	grande	gran-deh
small	piccolo	pee-koh-loh
hot	caldo	kal-doh
cold	freddo	fred-doh
good	buono	bwoh-noh
bad	cattivo	kat-tee-voh
enough	basta	bas-tah
well	bene	beh-neh
open	aperto	ah-pair-toh
closed	chiuso	kee-oo-zoh
left	a sinistra	ah see-nee-strah
right	a destra	ah dess-trah
straight on	sempre dritto	sem-preh dree-toh
near	vicino	vee-chee-noh
far	lontano	lon-tah-noh
up	su	soo
down	giù	joo
early	presto	press-toh
late	tardi	tar-dee
entrance	entrata	en-trah-tah
exit	uscita	oo-shee-ta
toilet	il gabinetto	eel gah-bee-net-toh
free, unoccupied	libero	lee-bair-oh
free, no charge	gratuito	grah-too-ee-toh
out of order	guasto	gwass-to
strike (train etc.)	sciopero	sho-pay-ro

MAKING A TELEPHONE CALL

I'd like to place a long-distance call.	Vorrei fare una interurbana.	vor-ray far-eh oona in-tair-oor-bah-nah
I'd like to make a reverse-charge call.	Vorrei fare una telefonata a carico del destinatario.	vor-ray far-eh oona teh-leh-fon-ah-tah a kar-ee-koh dell desstee-nah-tar-ree-oh
I'll try again later.	Ritelefono più tardi.	ree-teh-leh-foh-noh pee-oo tar-dee
Can I leave a message?	Posso lasciare un messaggio?	poss-oh lash-ah-reh oon mess-sah-joh?
Hold on.	Un attimo, per favore.	oon ah-tee-moh, pair fah-vor-eh
Could you speak up a little please?	Può parlare più forte, per favore?	pwoh par-lah-reh pee-oo for-teh, pair fah-vor-eh?
local call	la telefonata locale	lah teh-leh-fon-ah-ta loh-kah-leh

SHOPPING

How much does this cost?	Quant'è, per favore?	kwan-teh pair fah-vor-eh?
I would like ...	Vorrei...	vor-ray
Do you have ...?	Avete ...?	ah-veh-teh...?
I'm just looking.	Sto soltanto guardando.	stoh sol-tan-toh gwar-dan-doh
Do you take credit cards?	Accettate carte di credito?	ah-chet-tah-teh kar-teh dee creh-dee-toh?
What time do you open/close?	A che ora apre/ chiude?	ah keh or-ah ah-preh/kee-oo-deh?
this one	questo	kweh-stoh
that one	quello	kwell-oh
expensive	caro	kar-oh
cheap	a buon prezzo	ah bwon pret-soh
size, clothes	la taglia	lah tah-lee-ah
size, shoes	il numero	eel noo-mair-oh
white	bianco	bee-ang-koh
black	nero	neh-roh
red	rosso	ross-oh
yellow	giallo	jal-loh
green	verde	vair-deh
blue	blu/azzurro	bloo/at-zoo-row
brown	marrone	mar-roh-neh

TYPES OF SHOP

antique dealer	l'antiquario	lan-tee-kwah-ree-oh
bakery	la panetteria	lah pah-net-tair-ree-ah
bank	la banca	lah bang-kah
bookshop	la libreria	lah lee-breh-ree-ah
butcher's	la macelleria	lah mah-chell-eh-ree-ah
cake shop	la pasticceria	lah pas-tee-chair-ee-ah
chemist's	la farmacia	lah far-mah-chee-ah
delicatessen	la salumeria	lah sah-loo-meh ree-ah
department store	il grande magazzino	eel gran-deh mag-gad-zee-noh
fishmonger's	la pescheria	lah pess-keh-ree-ah
florist	il fioraio	eel fee-or-eye-oh
greengrocer	il fruttivendolo	eel froo-tee-ven-doh-loh
grocery	alimentari	ah-lee-men-tah-ree
hairdresser	il parrucchiere	eel par-oo-kee-air-eh
ice-cream parlour	la gelateria	lah jel-lah-tair-ree-ah
market	il mercato	eel mair-kah-toh
news-stand	l'edicola	leh-dee-koh-lah
post office	l'ufficio postale	loo-fee-choh pos-tah-leh
shoe shop	il negozio di scarpe	eel neh-goh-tsioh dee skar-peh
supermarket	il supermercato	su-pair-mair-kah-toh
tobacconist	il tabaccaio	eel tah-bak-eye-oh
travel agency	l'agenzia di viaggi	lah-jen-tsee-ah dee vee-ad-jee

SIGHTSEEING

art gallery	la pinacoteca	lah peena-koh-teh-kah
bus stop	la fermata dell'autobus	lah fair-mah-tah dell ow-toh-booss
church	la chiesa	lah kee-eh-zah
	la basilica	lah bah-seel-i-kah
closed for the public holiday	chiuso per la festa	kee-oo-zoh pair lah fess-tah
garden	il giardino	eel jar-dee-no
library	la biblioteca	lah beeb-lee-oh-teh-kah

museum	il museo	eel moo-zeh-oh
railway station	la stazione	lah stah-tsee-oh-neh
tourist information	l'ufficio turistico	loo-fee-choh too-ree-stee-koh

STAYING IN A HOTEL

Do you have any vacant rooms?	Avete camere libere?	ah-veh-teh kah-mair-eh lee-bair-eh?
double room	una camera doppia	oona kah-mair-ah doh-pee-ah
with double bed	con letto matrimoniale	kon let-toh mah-tree-moh-nee-ah-leh
twin room	una camera con due letti	oona kah-mair-ah kon doo-eh let-tee
single room	una camera singola	oona kah-mair-ah sing-goh-lah
room with a bath, shower	una camera con bagno, con doccia	oona kah-mair-ah kon ban-yoh, kon dot-chah
porter	il facchino	eel fah-kee-noh
key	la chiave	lah kee-ah-veh
I have a reservation.	Ho fatto una prenotazione.	oh fat-toh oona preh-noh-tah-tsee-oh-neh

EATING OUT

Have you got a table for ...?	Avete una tavola per ...?	ah-veh-teh oona tah-voh-lah pair ...?
I'd like to reserve a table.	Vorrei riservare una tavola.	vor-ray ree-sair-vah-reh oona tah-voh-lah
breakfast	colazione	koh-lah-tsee-oh-neh
lunch	pranzo	pran-tsoh
dinner	cena	cheh-nah
Enjoy your meal.	Buon appetito.	bwon ah-peh-tee-toh
The bill, please.	Il conto, per favore.	eel kon-toh pair fah-vor-eh
I am a vegetarian.	Sono vegetariano/a	ee-ah-noh/nah
waitress	cameriera	kah-mair-ee-air-ah
waiter	cameriere	kah-mair-ee-air-eh
fixed price menu	il menù a prezzo fisso	eel meh-noo ah pret-soh fee-soh
dish of the day	piatto del giorno	pee-ah-toh dell jor-no
starter	antipasto	an-tee-pass-toh
first course	il primo	eel pree-moh
main course	il secondo	eel seh-kon-doh
vegetables	il contorno	eel kon-tor-noh
dessert	il dolce	eel doll-cheh
cover charge	il coperto	eel koh-pair-toh
wine list	la lista dei vini	lah lee-stah day vee-nee
rare	al sangue	al sang-gweh
medium	al puntino	al poon-tee-noh
well done	ben cotto	ben kot-toh
glass	il bicchiere	eel bee-kee-air-eh
bottle	la bottiglia	lah bot-teel-yah
knife	il coltello	eel kol-tell-oh
fork	la forchetta	lah for-ket-tah
spoon	il cucchiaio	eel koo-kee-eye-oh

MENU DECODER

l'abbacchio	lah-back-kee-oh	lamb
l'aceto	lah-cheh-toh	vinegar
l'acqua	lah-kwah	water
l'acqua minerale	lah-kwah-mee-nair	mineral water
gasata/naturale	ah-leh gah-zah-tah/ nah-too rah-leh	fizzy/still
l'aglio	lahl-yoh	garlic
al forno	al for-noh	baked
alla griglia	ah-lah greel-yah	grilled
l'anatra	lah-nah-trah	duck
l'aragosta	lah-rah-goss-tah	lobster
l'arancia	lah-ran-chah	orange
arrosto	ar-ross-toh	roast
la birra	lah beer-rah	beer
la bistecca	lah bee-stek-kah	steak
il brodo	eel broh-doh	broth
il burro	eel boor-oh	butter
il caffè	eel kah-feh	coffee
il carciofo	eel kar-choff-oh	artichoke
la carne	la kar-neh	meat
carne di maiale	kar-neh dee mah-yah-leh	pork
la cipolla	lah chee-poll-ah	onion
i fagioli	ee fah-joh-lee	beans
il formaggio	eel for-mad-joh	cheese
le fragole	leh frah-goh-leh	strawberries
frutta fresca	froo-tah fress-kah	fresh fruit
frutti di mare	froo-tee dee mah-reh	seafood
i funghi	ee foon-gee	mushrooms

i gamberi	ee gam-bair-ee	prawns
il gelato	eel jel-lah-toh	ice cream
l'insalata	leen-sah-lah-tah	salad
il latte	eel laht-teh	milk
i legumi	ee leh-goo-mee	vegetables
lesso	less-oh	boiled
il manzo	eel man-tsoh	beef
la mela	lah meh-lah	apple
la melanzana	lah meh-lan-tsah-nah	aubergine
la minestra	lah mee-ness-trah	soup
l'olio	loll-yoh	oil
l'oliva	loh-lee-vah	olive
il pane	eel pah-neh	bread
il panino	eel pah-nee-noh	roll
le patate	leh pah-tah-teh	potatoes
patatine fritte	pah-tah-teen-eh free-teh	chips
il pepe	eel peh-peh	pepper
la pesca	lah pess-kah	peach
il pesce	eel pesh-eh	fish
il pollo	eel poll-oh	chicken
il pomodoro	eel poh-moh-dor-oh	tomato
il prosciutto cotto/crudo	eel pro-shoo-toh kot-toh/kroo-doh	ham cooked/cured
il riso	eel ree-zoh	rice
il sale	eel sah-leh	salt
la salsiccia	lah sal-see-chah	sausage
secco	sek-koh	dry
succo d'arancia/ di limone	soo-koh dah-ran-chah/ dee lee-moh-neh	orange/lemon juice
il tè	eel teh	tea
la tisana	lah tee-zah-nah	herb tea
il tonno	ton-noh	tuna
la torta	lah tor-tah	cake
l'uovo	loo-oh-voh	egg
l'uva	loo-vah	grapes
vino bianco	vee-noh bee-ang-koh	white wine
vino rosso	vee-noh ross-oh	red wine
il vitello	eel vee-tell-oh	veal
le vongole	leh von-goh-leh	baby clams
lo zucchero	loh zoo-kair-oh	sugar
gli zucchini	lyee dzo-kee-nee	courgettes
la zuppa	lah tsoo-pah	soup

NUMBERS

1	uno	oo-noh
2	due	doo-eh
3	tre	treh
4	quattro	kwat-roh
5	cinque	ching-kweh
6	sei	say-ee
7	sette	set-teh
8	otto	ot-toh
9	nove	noh-veh
10	dieci	dee-eh-chee
11	undici	oon-dee-chee
12	dodici	doh-dee-chee
13	tredici	tray-dee-chee
14	quattordici	kwat-tor-dee-chee
15	quindici	kwin-dee-chee
16	sedici	say-dee-chee
17	diciassette	dee-chah-set-teh
18	diciotto	dee-chot-toh
19	diciannove	dee-chah-noh-veh
20	venti	ven-tee
30	trenta	tren-tah
40	quaranta	kwah-ran-tah
50	cinquanta	ching-kwan-tah
60	sessanta	sess-an-tah
70	settanta	set-tan-tah
80	ottanta	ot-tan-tah
90	novanta	noh-van-tah
100	cento	chen-toh
1,000	mille	mee-leh
2,000	duemila	doo-eh mee-lah
5,000	cinquemila	ching-kweh mee-lah
1,000,000	un milione	oon meel- yoh-neh

TIME

one minute	un minuto	oon mee-noo-toh
one hour	un'ora	oon or-ah
half an hour	mezz'ora	medz-or-ah
a day	un giorno	oon jor-noh
a week	una settimana	oona set-tee-mah-nah
Monday	lunedì	loo-neh-dee
Tuesday	martedì	mar-teh-dee
Wednesday	mercoledì	mair-koh-leh-dee
Thursday	giovedì	joh-veh-dee
Friday	venerdì	ven-air-dee
Saturday	sabato	sah-bah-toh
Sunday	domenica	doh-meh-nee-kah

ACKNOWLEDGMENTS

The publisher would like to thank the following for their kind permission to reproduce their photographs:

Key: a-above; b-below/bottom; c-centre; f-far; l-left; r-right; t-top

4Corners: Paolo Evangelista 76-77b, Maurizio Rellini 50b, 160cb, Massimo Ripani 33br, Alessandro Saffo 77cra

Alamy Stock Photo: Agencja Fotograficzna Caro / caro 44tr, AGF Srl / Luca Dadi 128crb, Album 87cla, 159tc, Frank Bach 77cla, Antonio Balasco 20cr, blickwinkel / McPHOTO / O. Protze 33t, Alessandro Bosio 110cra, Federico Calvani 36bl, Michele Castellani 8clb, Classic Image 55bl, ClickAlps Srls 68-69t, Roy Conchie 82-83t, Ian Dagnall 57cra, 109cra, Danita Delimont / Julie Eggers 48tl, Pavel Dudek 152t, Madeleine Duquenne 90-91b, Adam Eastland 18crb, 34-35t, 45crb, 81tl, 130clb, Sergio Feola 107bc, freeartist 170-171t, Gacro74 75cra, Manfred Gottschalk 20cl, Bertolissio Giovanni / Hemis.fr 165br, 166-167, Historic Collection 54bl, Image Professionals GmbH / LOOK-foto 149tl, Image Professionals GmbH / Ulli Seer 41tr, imageBROKER.com GmbH & Co. KG / Ronald Wittek 149ca, Imago / Cheng Tingting 52crb, IMAGO / Jin Mamengni 43br, Imago / Jin Yu 53cl, Independent Photo Agency Srl 83cr, INTERFOTO / Personalities 109tl, Ivoha 109tr, Jon Arnold Images Ltd / Peter Adams 8-9b, Wolfgang Kaehler 10clb, 39cl, 51br, 52cl, Joana Kruse 47t, 77tr, 104-105t, Theodore Liasi 47br, Elio Lombardo 29c, De Luan 57tl, mauritius images GmbH / ClickAlps 12t, mauritius images GmbH / Otmar Steinbicker 96clb, Emanuele Mazzoni 22bl, MB_Photo 138b, Angus McComiskey 83bl, David Meggitt 42tl, Valerio Mei 26br, 156-157t, Russell Mountford 18bl, Old Images 54t, Guido Paradisi 41clb, 80bl, 84clb, 85cra, 88-89, Paolo Paradiso 40tl, 51t, Igor Prahin 22cr, 64bl, RealyEasyStar / Claudio Pagliarani 18cr, 86cla, REDA &CO srl 24cl, 52cr, 67crb, 104bc, 138clb, REDA &CO srl / GGR 18t, REDA &CO srl / Michele Bella 11br, Robert Harding 69crb, robertharding / ProCip 13cr, Grant Rooney 48-49b, Johan Siebke 143, Nicola Simeoni 116-117b, Witold Skrypczak 103br, Stock Italia 43cl, Gabriele Thielmann 66tr, Mauro Toccaceli 24bl, 53tr, 66-67b, 76bl, 140tr, travelbild-Italy 129tl, Giovanni Mereghetti / UCG / Universal Images Group 32br, Universal Images Group North America LLC / marka / nevio doz 40cra, wanderluster 46-47bc, Westend61 GmbH 22crb, 40b, 41br, Westend61 GmbH / Lorenzo Mattei 94

AWL Images: ClickAlps 2-3, 26t, 28bl, 42-43b, 52clb, 114-115t, 141b, Michele Falzone 124-125t, Francesco Iacobelli 10-11bc, 11t, 12-13b, 50tl, 58-59, 160-161, 164-165t, 168t, Tim Mannakee 148-149b, Ken Scicluna 78-79b, Ian Trower 150-151t, Catherina Unger 8cla, 30-31b

Bridgeman Images: © Fototeca Inasa / NPL - DeA Picture Library 54cb, © Galleria Nazionale dell'Umbria 56cb, Fototeca Gilardi 57tr

Camera Etrusca: Patrick Richmond Nicholas 44b

Depositphotos Inc: Dziurek 46tl

Dreamstime.com: Leonid Andronov 71t, Bernard Bialorucki 16c, 60-61, 126tr, 131cra, Crisfotolux 91tr, Dmfrancesco 45cla, Lorenzo Dottorini 116tl, Dudlajzov 73tr, 105br, 153bl,

Main Contributors Toni DeBella,
Marina Dragoni, Giovanni Francesio,
Elizabeth Heath, Patrizia Masnini
Senior Editors Dipika Dasgupta, Zoë Rutland
Senior Designer Vinita Venugopal
Project Editors Rachel Laidler,
Anuroop Sanwalia
Editor Aimee White
Assistant Editors Nandini Desiraju, Anjasi N.N
Assistant Art Editor Divyanshi Shreyaskar
Proofreader Kathryn Glendenning
Indexer Helen Peters
Senior Picture Researcher Nishwan Rasool
Picture Research Manager Taiyaba Khatoon
Assistant Picture Research Administrator
Manpreet Kaur
Publishing Assistant Simona Velikova
Jacket Designers Jordan Lambley,
Divyanshi Shreyaskar
Cartography Manager Suresh Kumar
Cartographer Ashif Ashif
Senior DTP Designer Tanveer Zaidi
Senior Production Controller Samantha Cross
Managing Editors Shikha Kulkarni,
Beverly Smart, Hollie Teague
Managing Art Editor Priyanka Thakur
Art Director Maxine Pedliham
Publishing Director Georgina Dee

First edition 2004

Published in Great Britain by Dorling Kindersley Limited,
DK, One Embassy Gardens, 8 Viaduct Gardens,
London SW11 7BW, UK

The authorised representative in the EEA is
Dorling Kindersley Verlag GmbH. Arnulfstr.
124, 80636 Munich, Germany

Published in the United States by DK Publishing,
1745 Broadway, 20th Floor, New York, NY 10019, USA

Copyright © 2004, 2024 Dorling Kindersley Limited
A Penguin Random House Company

24 25 26 27 10 9 8 7 6 5 4 3 2 1

The publishers cannot accept responsibility for any consequences
arising from the use of this book, nor for any material on third
party websites, and cannot guarantee that any website address in
this book will be a suitable source of travel information.

A CIP catalog record for this book
is available from the British Library.

A catalog record for this book is available
from the Library of Congress.

ISSN: 1542 1554
ISBN: 978 0 2416 7072 9

Printed and bound in China.

www.dk.com

A NOTE FROM DK EYEWITNESS

The rate at which the world is changing is constantly
keeping the DK Eyewitness team on our toes. While
we've worked hard to ensure that this edition of
DK Eyewitness Umbria is accurate and up-to-date, we
know that opening hours alter, standards shift, prices
fluctuate, places close and new ones pop up in their
stead. So, if you notice we've got something wrong or
left something out, we want to hear about it.
Please get in touch at travelguides@dk.com